Noncoherent Optical Processing

WILEY SERIES IN PURE AND APPLIED OPTICS

Advisory Editor
Stanley S. Ballard, University of Florida

ALLEN AND EBERLY • *Optical Resonance and Two-Level Atoms*

BABCOCK • *Silicate Glass Technology Methods*

BOND • *Crystal Technology*

CATHEY • *Optical Information Processing and Holography*

CAULFIELD AND LU • *The Applications of Holography*

GERRARD AND BURCH • *Introduction to Matrix Methods in Optics*

HUDSON • *Infrared System Engineering*

JUDD AND WYSZECKI • *Color in Business, Science, and Industry*, Third Edition

KNITTL • *Optics of Thin Films*

LENGYEL • *Lasers, Second Edition*

LEVI • *Applied Optics, A Guide to Optical System Design*, Volume I

LOUISELL • *Quantum Statistical Properties of Radiation*

MCCARTNEY • *Optics of the Atmosphere; Scattering by Molecules and Particles*

MOLLER AND ROTHSCHILD • *Far-Infrared Spectroscopy*

PRATT • *Laser Communication Systems*

ROGERS • *Noncoherent Optical Processing*

SHULMAN • *Optical Data Processing*

WILLIAMS AND BECKLUND • *Optics*

ZERNIKE AND MIDWINTER • *Applied Nonlinear Optics*

Noncoherent
Optical Processing

G. L. ROGERS

**University of Aston in Birmingham,
Great Britain**

John Wiley & Sons, New York / London / Sydney / Toronto

Library of Congress Cataloging in Publication Data

Rogers, Gordon Leonard, 1916–
  Noncoherent optical processing.

  (Wiley series in pure and applied optics)
  Includes bibliographies and index.
  1. Optical data processing. I. Title.

TA1632.R63   621.36   77-5453
ISBN 0-471-73055-6

Printed in the United States of America

10 9 8 7 6 5 4 3 2 1

To My Wife

Preface

Since the invention of the laser there has been a great development of coherent optical processing techniques and an explosion of books dealing with them. Among these books are E. L. O'Neil's *Introduction to Statistical Optics*, and J. W. Goodman's *Introduction to Fourier Optics*, which deal with the basic theory. A number of recent books concentrate on holography, but add significant sections on other types of coherent image processing. To cite only two, we can mention the work of Cathey and Yu. There is also a substantial work by Schulman called *Optical Data Processing*, which is exclusively devoted to coherent optical data processing.

All this activity has tended to obscure a parallel development in the field of noncoherent optics. The Zernike-Van Cittert theorem allows us to develop a noncoherent or partially coherent system analogous to any coherent system that operates on a wholly real object (i.e., an object which does not introduce phase changes on the coherent beam passing through it). From time to time conscious use is made of this theorem to develop new noncoherent or partially coherent techniques such as entrance pupil filters, mentioned in Chapter 10 and Appendix V. Other techniques were suggested by the theorem, but proved to be simple devices that can be explained in geometrical terms, such as the spatial frequency filter.

The problem with coherent optical processes lies in its vulnerability to noise. Consequently, the results tend to be disappointing, if applied, for example, to a blurred photograph not processed under laboratory control and subject to grain noise and nonuniformity of grain. A study of redundancy shows that most of such systems are nonredundant and hence one error entering the system can never be removed. Noncoherent systems tend to be heavily redundant, the same basic information being carried in many parallel channels, so that an error in one channel will make little impact on the output, which is the average of the many channels. On the other hand, the total information handling capacity of the system is correspondingly reduced.

The second problem is the inability of noncoherent systems to handle negative numbers. The immediate answer to this is to add a DC bias to make all the numbers positive. But this reduces the overall contrast of the image, and ordinary visual inspection has to be supplemented by special techniques for spatial and temporal modulation. The development in these techniques in the past 15 years has been quite remarkable.

This book has, therefore, been written to draw attention to these developments and to provide a theoretical basis for what might otherwise appear to be disconnected efforts. At the same time it is confidently expected that the explicit statement of these principles will encourage new developments and greatly assist the design of such systems.

I am indebted to Messrs Macmillan and Company for permission to reproduce Figure 1.4; to the editors of *Sky and Telescope* and Drs. Mertz and Young for the use of Figures 7.2 and 7.3; and to I.P.C., the publishers of *Optics and Laser Technology* and its editor for permission to use some of the diagrams in my August 1975 article. I am also much indebted to Mrs. D. G. Hill for her patience with the typing and Mr. A. Mackenzie for drawing the diagrams and taking the photograph of Figure 1.1. The complex grids shown in Figures 8.11 and 10.2 were constructed by Mr. B. Brookes.

G. L. ROGERS

Birmingham, Great Britain
March 1977

Contents

Noncoherent Optical Processing

1

Historical Introduction

Noncoherent optical processes use ordinary white light that occurs outside the laboratory. Coherent light, which has come into prominence in the last two or three decades, is a very artificial phenomenon. The nearest thing to it in nature is the wavefront from a single star, which is both very weak and mixed up with the wavefronts of many other stars. A beam of sunlight is coherent over only a small fraction of a millimeter sideways and a few micrometers longitudinally. In fact, the lateral coherence distance in sunlight is so small that we can compare it to the separation of the lenslets of an insect compound eye.

Ordinary sources are characterized by a wide range of wavelengths: even a strongly colored pigment will normally reflect a range of wavelengths some 10% of its peak value. The sources are also of finite size and are often diffuse. Much optical information is gathered by the eye through reflection from diffuse surfaces of considerable angular size that may have information written or printed on them. Noncoherent optical processing consists of devising methods to assist the eye in interpreting input data in such a form.

1.1. THE STEREOSCOPE AND THE WINKER

An early device for comparing two closely similar pictures or diagrams was the stereoscope, invented by Wheatstone (1838). Originally this device used two photographs or drawings of a three-dimensional scene taken from slightly different angles. Later the instrument was used for a variety of purposes, including aerial surveys.

1

A particular application of this instrument was to detect changes between two patterns. This is a useful aspect of data processing wherein a large amount of information (the constant term) is rejected and the relevant information (the change) is selected out. If the change is small compared with the constant term, direct examination can be very time-consuming and subject to human error.

If the two patterns are put in a stereoscope, the constant terms lock to give a flat (two-dimensional) picture, because they are identical and show no parallax. The differences in the pattern now become apparent as regions where the pattern fails to lock. Very often the changed element will appear to float round in space; for example, it may appear nearer or farther away than the background. The impression is, however, psychologically unsatisfactory and one has a sense of strain as one scans the defective region. Such regions can be marked and studied in further detail. A skilled operator will pick up half a dozen changes in seconds, whereas detailed direct comparisons may require minutes. It is a technique often used in children's columns in the newspaper where one is asked to "spot the difference" between similar pictures. It can also be used in the detection of forgeries.

The use of a stereoscope makes demands on the skill of the observer and, because not all observers are equally gifted with stereoscopic vision, this technique has fallen into disuse. It has been replaced by the winker, which is a device with a system of mirrors and a lever that allows an optical path to be switched from one picture to another. In this case the picture can be viewed with a single eye, although instruments with a beam splitter and binocular eyepiece are available. The constant terms in the picture are adjusted so they do not shift when the lever is swung over but the changes appear to move by contrast with the fixed background. Instruments of this type are widely used in comparing star photographs to detect planetary movements.

1.2. THE PERIODOGRAM

A very crude method of optical data processing that has led to many developments of one kind or another was introduced by Sir Arthur Schuster in 1898 (Schuster 1898). Schuster was concerned with a number of geophysical problems including terrestrial magnetism. The method he developed is a way of determining whether magnetic phenomena have any cyclic periodicities. For example, let us suppose we wished to test magnetic data for a possible lunar cycle of 29 days.

In Schuster's procedure the numbers (or crude symbols representing their magnitudes in a set of steps) are set in rows of daily observations 29 days long. Then a new row is started. In this way observations stretching over many years are set out in strips one lunar month long. If there *is* a relationship between the lunar month and the magnetic data one will tend to get vertical columns of either high or low values. If not the values will scatter uniformly and no pattern will emerge. The presence of vertical columns will indicate that if, for instance, a high value tends to occur on day 12 of the first row, it will recur on day 12 of the second row, day 12 of the third row, and so forth, and a high value will be found on a column 12 places in from the left-hand edge.

A refinement of this technique takes into account the possibility that the phenomenon has periodicity different from that anticipated. Suppose, for instance, one sets out the data in rows 29 days long in anticipation of a lunar period, but that the period is actually 28 days. In this case, the high value occurring on day 12 of the first row is followed by a high on day 11 of the second row and on day 10 of the third row and so forth. In this case the data will tend to form *oblique* lines.

1.3. THE DOUGLASS CYLINDRICAL LENS TECHNIQUE

A. E. Douglass (1914, 1915) used the idea of the periodogram to develop a piece of equipment that is the first processor specially built to examine noncoherent optical data I have been able to trace. It differs from previous methods because the data are set out, not in number form, but in analogue form. They are represented by plotting the data vertically against a horizontal time axis. The resulting curve is represented as a white area of variable height on a black background. For example, it may be cut out of a white sheet of paper and stuck onto a black sheet.

Sections of the curve are now arranged above one another so that the length of each section is an integral multiple of one of the supposed periods. In this way, we should expect to get vertical stripes: if, however, the estimated period is slightly in error we get oblique stripes.

To pick out vertical stripes, the whole pattern is now viewed or photographed through a cylindrical lens with its cylinder axis vertical.

This causes blurring in a vertical direction, but focuses on a screen or plate in a horizontal direction. Vertical stripes thus give rise to a high-contrast vertical pattern.

In order to seek for other periodicities represented by oblique stripes we must now rotate either the lens or the pattern about a horizontal axis perpendicular to the plane of the input data; Douglass chose to rotate the pattern. In a refinement he used a narrow horizontal slit in front of the photographic plate and almost in its plane. While he rotated the pattern he moved the photographic plate vertically past the slit. In this way different horizontal strips at different vertical heights on the plate corresponded to different periodicities in the data. Strong periodicities gave good fringes which fade away where there is no corresponding periodicity in the data. Figure 1.1 shows a student experiment based on the Douglass principle. In this case, the camera has a cylindrical lens

Figure 1.1 Photograph of student experiment on the Douglass principle. The periodic structure is cut up into strips and placed on a rotating stand. A camera with a cylindrical lens blurs the picture along the cylinder axis (here horizontal). Twisting the input in its own plane brings various frequencies "in tune" and gives a sharp "image" on the viewing screen. Illumination is by diffuse white light.

with its cylinder axis horizontal. The input pattern showing a number of strips of synthetic data is mounted in a rotating frame. The input pattern was computed to contain three basic periodicities not simply related.

Douglass also called his output a periodogram, because different vertical heights correspond to different periodicities. It will be seen that this is quite a sophisticated machine incorporating a number of different ideas. One is Schuster's periodogram for the detection of frequency. Another very useful device is the cylindrical lens. When used with a single strip of variable area data, the cylindrical lens converts it into a variable density record. A similar technique has been used to produce an artificial hologram from a calculated diffraction pattern plotted as a variable area record (Rogers 1952).

1.4. FOSTER'S SHADOWGRAPH METHOD

Foster (1930) described a shadowgraph to detect periodicities. This resembles the cylindrical lens technique in that the shadowgraph also introduces blurring in one direction—here vertical. Just as a pinhole camera may be regarded as a limiting case of a camera with a spherical lens, a single slit has imaging properties analogous to a cylindrical lens, focusing in one direction and blurring in the direction at right angles. Such a device, like a pinhole, lacks photographic speed. To overcome this difficulty, Foster used an array of regularly spaced slits. This introduces a new factor. While a pinhole or slit system has unlimited focal depth, so that it will form an image at any distance, the array produces overlapping images, which blur unless the distance at which they are formed happens to "lock" with a spatial frequency in the input pattern. An array of slits, therefore, selectively images each input frequency at a different distance. In order to make use of this, Foster puts his array of slits in a plane inclined to the input plane and to the output or "focusing" plane. Different frequencies now "focus" at different heights (Figure 1.2).

The Foster shadowgraph has since been developed into a very useful spatial frequency filter (Leifer et al. 1969). The purpose of this is to isolate a spatial frequency from an input pattern and detect it electronically. Since the electronic detector works best when coupled to a single-frequency filter, the shadowing grid is held parallel to the input

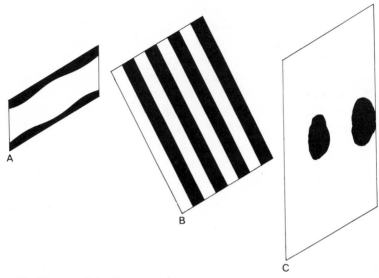

Figure 1.2 Diagram of the Foster periodogram experiment. The input A interacts with an inclined shadowing grid B, so that a sharp shadow is only formed on the viewing screen C at a particular height characteristic of that particular frequency. The input function must not be too high. If the function contains a number of frequencies, there will be a number of sharp shadows at varying heights with diffuse regions in between.

and output planes. Different frequencies can be accommodated by running a number of single-frequency filters in parallel.

1.5. LENTICULAR FILM COLOR PHOTOGRAPHY

Mention was made above of the possibility of running data-processing units in parallel. This starts as an exercise in data-handling, wherein data is coded and stored in a special form to allow for compression. There have been a number of early attempts to compress two or more stereoscopic viewpoints into a single picture by using line screens or lenticular grids to chop the data up into strips and present the viewpoints successively by parallax as the observer moves around. A full history of these developments would be beyond the scope of this book. Fortunately, the subject has been well treated by Dudley (1951) to whom readers are referred.

As a particular example of the use of a lenticular grid system, we outline a process of color photography that was developed commercially for color-cine work in the early 1930s.

The object has a slowly varying polar diagram in its emission (Figure 1.3). Thus if the imaging lens is split up into three regions by the use of a color filter, we shall receive essentially the same outlines of the object through each of the three filters. We now "process" the input data in each channel by examining its spectral luminosity with a color filter, thereby extracting certain information. These processing operations occur at the same time and are therefore "in parallel."

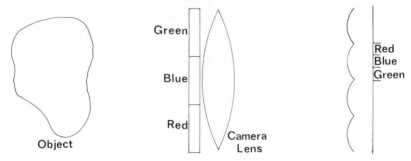

Figure 1.3 Parallel processing. The old "Kodacolor" process involves the parallel processing of the image through three separate channels produced by the triple filter over the taking lens and kept separate by the filter image in each lenticulation of the taking film.

Having separated the data we must be careful that they do not get confused again at a later date. If the camera lens were focused onto an ordinary photographic film this would, of course, occur—the three channels would be brought to focus at the same image point. A special lenticular recording film is therefore used which focuses light from the three separate parts of the main lens onto different strips in the emulsion coat on the back surface of the film. The lenticulations, which run at 1000 to the inch, have a front curvature which makes the emulsion surface lie in their focal plane.

We are now faced with the problem of recovering the information. The emulsion used is panchromatic but it yields a black and white image. For convenience, this is reversal processed. The colors have now to be reintroduced in the projection process. Fortunately, this can be done by using the principle of reversibility of rays. The projector light is shone first through the picture on the back of the film and then through the lenticular grating. This separates the information into three fans or bundles passing through different regions of the projection lens. We can now place a composite color filter over the projector lens and reintroduce the appropriate color into each separate fan.

The process is light-additive, as opposed to the more commonly used dye-subtractive methods. It is, therefore, rather inefficient in its use of light. A further complication is that the lenticular base has to be matched in acceptance angle with the angular aperture of the camera lens. The latter must, therefore, always be used at full aperture in the horizontal plane. Special stops have to be used on the system in bright light.

1.6. THE BRAGG–HUGGINS MASKS

X-ray crystallography involves a great deal of data handling. The relative intensities of the various X-ray reflections that can be obtained from a single crystal are related to the crystal structure by a Fourier transform, being proportional to its squared modulus. Conversely, it is theoretically possible to calculate the crystal structure from the X-ray data provided the phases can be correctly inferred. These transforms can be reduced to two- or three-dimensional scans of a set of Fourier series. In the early days, only two-dimensional scans could be attempted, and they were chosen to represent projections of the matter in a crystal unit cell onto a suitable crystallographic plane.

Calculations were often performed numerically. To avoid the tedium of this procedure, a number of analogue methods were developed.

Sir Lawrence Bragg (1929) devised a system of using a sheet of bromide paper to add up the sine waves for him. Photographic masks were prepared of different spacings and orientations, and they were projected successively onto the same sheet of bromide paper. The exposure of each mask was then adjusted in relation to the X-ray intensity of the corresponding reflection. The bromide paper was assumed to have a linear relationship between exposure and resulting density and, on development, gave the structure of the crystal projected onto the chosen plane. Huggins (1941) subsequently produced a set of masks on a strip of 35mm film which was very convenient. The procedure was made obsolete by refinements in computing techniques and is now out of use (Figure 1.4).

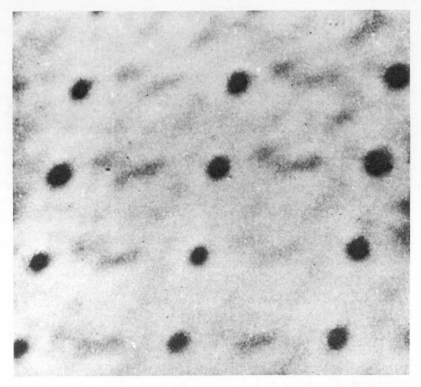

Figure 1.4 A noncoherent crystallographic reconstruction due to W. L. Bragg.

1.7. CALCULATION OF PATTERSON PROJECTIONS

The X-ray crystallographers continued their use of noncoherent optical processing techniques even after the original Fourier transform was being obtained by calculation or by coherent techniques. In particular, a procedure was developed that did not require knowledge of the X-ray phases. Projections were calculated from the X-ray intensities directly instead of from the X-ray amplitudes. It is now well known that if you multiply a Fourier transform by itself, that is, if you square all the coefficients, you get the transform of the convolution of the original pattern with itself. Now the use of X-ray intensities is, of course, equivalent to squaring the original transform. The artificial projection so obtained, called a Patterson projection after its originator, is thus the autoconvolution of the crystal structure. As in the early days crystal-

lographers tended to choose centrosymmetrical crystals, this autoconvolution is equivalent to an autocorrelation.

It is fairly easy to sketch the projection of a number of atoms in a trial
structure on paper, but it becomes tedious to calculate their autocorrelation pattern since n atoms give rise to $n(n-1)$ spots (aside from the
central one). The procedure generally employed was to cut holes in a
black mask representing the trial structure and make two copies of it. In
one arrangement, one copy was half the size of the other; the larger
copy was set in contact with a diffuse light source and the smaller
halfway between it and the recording photographic plate. A dense spot
was then recorded at the center of the plate, where each spot correlates
with itself on the smaller copy, surrounded with a whole array of
cross-correlation spots (Haag 1944).

An interesting variation on this theme is to use a set of light bulbs to
represent the atoms in the first plane and a set of opaque spherical
obstructions to represent them on a reduced scale in the second plane.
One then gets a set of shadows on the plane of convergence. Since each
light bulb may be connected with an elastic cord to its corresponding
opaque obstruction and this in turn can be connected with an elastic
cord to a common point of convergence, an adjustable system can be
produced. Any particular atom can now be moved around: its corresponding obstruction follows it and the resulting Patterson projection
can be compared with the calculated pattern (Robertson 1943).

1.8. LONG-RANGE DETECTION OF INSECTS

Although not an obvious case of noncoherent processing, the work of
Richards (1955) in detecting insects was an early use of temporal
modulation in the processing of an optical signal. In view of the central
position that temporal modulation occupies in the field of noncoherent
data processing, this early evidence of its great sensitivity is very
interesting.

Richards was exploring a system for light-beam telephony and tested
his receiver by allowing the sun to fall directly onto his photocell. The
cell was connected to an ac amplifier which suppressed the constant
term in the cell current. He found that light clouds passing over the sun
produced a low-pitched rumble, but he also observed short pings lasting
0.1 to 0.25 seconds with frequencies ranging from 100 to 500 Hz. To

determine whether these pings represented insects, Richards set up two independent receivers side by side and from time to time got correlated pings with a slight time delay; that is, when an insect flies from one light path to the other. He estimated speeds of 5 to 10 miles per hour and got signals when no insect was visible or audible. The observations were checked by trapping an insect in a glass-sided cell and putting it in the beam.

The cone of light from the sun to the photocell is fairly narrow but, nevertheless, an insect does not interrupt much of it. The ac signals produced by the insect therefore represent a very small ripple on the DC level of the light. The fact that they can be detected demonstrates that temporal modulation techniques are very sensitive and can detect output signals that are invisible to the naked eye.

REFERENCES

Bragg, W. L. (1929). *Zeitschr. Krist.* **70**, 475.

Douglass, A. E. (1914). *Astrophys. J.* **40**, 326–331.

Douglass, A. E. (1915). *Astrophys. J.* **41**, 173–186.

Dudley, L. P. (1951). *Stereoptics*, Macdonald & Co, London.

Foster, G. A. R. (1930), *J. Test. Inst.* **21**, T18.

Haag, G. (1944). *Nature (GB)* **153**, 81.

Huggins, M. L. (1941). *J. Amer. Chem. Soc.* **63**, 66.

Leifer, I., G. L. Rogers, and N. W. F. Stephens (1969). *Opt. Acta* **16**, 535–553.

Richards, I. R. (1955). *Nature (GB)* **175**, 128–9.

Robertson, J. M. (1943). *Nature (GB)* **152**, 411.

Rogers, G. L. (1952). *Proc. Roy. Soc. Edinb.* (A) **63**, 313.

Schuster, A. (1898). *Terr. Magn.* **3**, 13–41.

Wheatstone, C. (1838). *Phil. Trans. Roy. Soc. (GB)* P + I, 371–394.

2

The Extended
Luminous Source

Noncoherent optical data processing starts with an extended diffuse luminous source. Because the source is laterally extended, the system lacks lateral coherence, and, by the use of white light, any longitudinal coherence can be reduced to negligible limits. For descriptive purposes, it is convenient to regard the source as uniform, and attribute any variation of intensity to a variable transparency placed in contact with it. This double system of uniform source and contact transparency can be made to simulate any of the other practical arrangements in common use.

For example, we may use a diffusely reflecting sheet of white paper, uniformly illuminated from the front, with some of the input information on it in the form of printed signs. Again it may be a "coded source" of the type used in X-ray and γ-ray systems to increase the effective speed of the apparatus and provide an element of depth discrimination. It could be a screen with an image projected onto it, or it could be the output of a television system—a cathode ray tube displaying a variation of luminous intensity. The cathode ray tube output could be a continuously scanned picture, or it could be a diagram drawn by an alphanumeric scanner in a programmed sequence. In both cases, the time taken to complete a scan becomes a limiting factor in the speed of the system, and the scan characteristics will impose limitations on the use of temporal modulation in the processor.

2.1. CHARACTERISTICS OF A DIFFUSE SOURCE

The principal characteristic of a diffuse source is that if two small areas are chosen arbitrarily, their polar diagrams will have very similar shapes. The scale of the diagrams may vary; the brighter of the two areas will have a larger polar diagram than the darker, but it will be a scaled up version of the darker polar diagram. Moreover, in the type of source particularly suited to optical data processing, the polar diagram shape will be broad. A Lambertian source is easily realized and very useful; that is, one with a flux I_θ at an angle θ to the surface normal given by

$$I_\theta = I_0 \cos \theta \dagger$$

where I_0 is the flux in the normal direction.

It will be seen that I_θ does not vary from I_0 by more than 6% as θ varies $\pm 20°$ from the normal. This means that the intensity is nearly constant over a useful range of angles.

The typical source will then carry information in the form of variations in I_0 as the surface is scanned, but the shape of the polar diagrams involved will vary little. The variation with (x, y) displacements over the source can be very rapid, corresponding to a pattern with fine detail. But angular variations will be very slow. Thus the basic pattern can be seen from a number of different viewpoints, subject to a small projective distortion, and different optical processes can be performed on the pattern simultaneously by arranging the processing units around the surface normal. This we call parallel processing, and we treat it in the next chapter.

2.2. INPUT SYSTEMS

As mentioned above, we can represent any source by using a uniform diffuse source plus a transparency. This is a handy way to construct an input, because of its flexibility. The source is conveniently a translucent

†Strictly speaking a noncoherent source has a law $I_\theta = I_0 \cos^2 \theta$ (see Carter and Wolf 1975). This is more difficult to construct. The two sources differ principally in the region where two coherence sampling points are close together. If they are separated by 10 wavelengths or more the differences are unimportant. Since it is a basic assumption of this work that none of the input transparencies have detail anywhere near the diffraction limit it is legitimate to use the more easily constructed Lambertian source.

one, with a slot for inserting the transparency in front of it. In practice one usually makes the gap between the source and transparency fairly small, although in principle they can be separated by some distance, provided the source is bigger than the transparency so that it is uniformly illuminated from all the angles of view.

For simple experiments, a useful light box can be made by illuminating a piece of opal glass from behind with a single lamp placed a distance of at least twice the source diagonal away from the opal glass. Even with a point source in a black box, the corners of the opal glass are only 10% darker than the center. By the use of a pearl lamp of finite size and by painting the internal surfaces of the box white, this discrepancy can be greatly reduced, and sources of this type are in regular use in our laboratory.

When using an input printed on paper it is necessary to illuminate from the same side as the observer or apparatus. A single source is thus not very convenient, because it obscures the line of view. To solve this problem, four lamps of equal power can be placed at the corners of a square, and the plane is viewed through the center of the square. To achieve the most uniform illumination, the side of the square must be correctly related to the distance of the lamps from the illuminated plane. If the side of the square is $2a$, and h is the distance of the plane of the lamps from the illuminated plane we have to adjust h so that

$$3a^2 > h^2 > 2a^2$$

The upper limit corresponds to a system where the center region is more strongly illuminated than the edges and corners by some 10%. If, however, one is only concerned with a relatively small area near the center, up to 36% of the total area, the illumination is very uniform. The lower limit corresponds to the case where the center is less well illuminated than the edges or corners, again by roughly 10%. In between it is difficult to calculate analytically the positions of minimum and maximum illumination. The matter is examined further in Appendix III.

The effort required to achieve a uniformly illuminated source is well worthwhile, because many of the procedures used in optical data processing involve very high-contrast reproduction of the final output, and nonuniformities in the source are greatly exaggerated. The required output can therefore be distorted unless the source is very uniform to begin with.

2.3. POTENTIAL INFORMATION-CARRYING CAPACITY OF THE SOURCE

As shown in Appendix II, the information-carrying capacity of an optical system, considered as a whole, is subject to a diffraction limit of $(Etendu)/\lambda^2$. The Etendu takes into account not only the size of the source but also the angular aperture of the observing system. The amount of information that can usefully be fed into the source, therefore, depends on the mode of observation.

Nevertheless, it is highly desirable not to feed into the input anything approaching the theoretical maximum of information. This means that the system has redundancy; that is, it is carrying the input information several or many times over in parallel channels. This in turn makes it resistant to noise. It is well-known that coherent systems, which are frequently nonredundant, are easily upset by the presence of dust or small disturbing particles.

Parallel processing is also possible because some of the informational redundancy can be traded off against multiple working. Both these effects are discussed in the next chapter. The case of parallel processing can also be treated by using the angular size of one unit in the processor when calculating the Etendu and then allowing a factor of safety to produce redundancy.

2.4. NEGATIVE NUMBERS: THE USE OF DC BIAS

The main limitation on noncoherent optical processing is that it works with luminous intensities, and intensities can only be added. It is, therefore, not possible to represent directly a function with both positive and negative values. Such a function must be transformed arbitrarily so that it is always positive. The simplest way to achieve this transformation is to find some positive number that is greater than the modulus of the most negative value of the function within the range being studied. If this constant is then added to all values of the function it will produce an input that is everywhere positive. The procedure is essentially arbitrary because a search must first be made to find the most negative value before the positive constant is added. This constant is analogous to a dc bias in electronics and is consequently called the DC bias. (In this book capitals are used for optical signals and lowercase for electrical signals.)

There are a number of drawbacks to this technique. The first and most obvious is that the range of variation is artificially reduced and the contrast of the output is reduced accordingly. Other complications arise when one combines one input function with another, because the DC bias of each function is not necessarily the same. The cross products of these DC biases will also produce a swamping effect on the output. The DC bias in the output will often be a good deal higher than the figure just necessary to avoid negative values in the output. This further reduces the contrast of the output, and hence contrast-enhancing photographic or electronic techniques become necessary. These, in turn, demand enhanced uniformity of the input sources.

The effect of DC bias is calculated in Chapter 4 in the practically important case of an optical correlator.

2.5. INPUTTING A SECOND PIECE OF INFORMATION

The first input transparency is normally placed very close to the diffuse source, but we may now insert a second transparency some way from it: ideally at a distance that is large when compared with the lateral dimensions of the apparatus. This gives rise to a very interesting situation. Imagine first that there is a small region in the second transparency which is a good deal lighter than its immediate surroundings and then consider the polar diagram just behind it. The light region will act as a pinhole camera, so that the polar diagram will give a pinhole image of the source. In other words, its shape will reflect the information in the first transparency. The polar diagrams just behind other points in the second transparency will be of similar shapes but will have different sizes or scales. Information about the second transparency is thus obtained by averaging each individual polar diagram over direction. This can be done, for example, by placing a photographic plate in contact with the second transparency and making a contact print. Such a print is independent of the structure of the first transparency. To isolate information about the structure of the first transparency we must find a polar diagram that is averaged over the area of the second transparency. This can be done by placing a lens immediately behind the second transparency and photographing the first transparency. This argument assumes that neither transparency contains information at anything like the diffraction limit; that is that the system has high redundancy.

A system of two planes, where the information is separable in the above sense, has been studied in detail by Dorrestein (1950). He calls the two planes "independent planes" and shows that in an imaging system each plane generates a set of conjugate planes. Any of two of these conjugate planes, one from each set, will be independent. The author prefers to call these independent planes "orthogonal planes" and refers to orthogonality in an optical system.

For the benefit of readers trained in mathematics and for the convenience of those who are not, a detailed matrix treatment of these ideas is isolated in Appendix I.

REFERENCES

Carter, W. H. and E. Wolf (1975). *J. Opt. Soc. Amer.* **65**, 1067.
Dorrestein, R. (1950). *Philips Res. Rep.* **5**, 116.

3

Parallel Processing
and Redundancy

The possibility of parallel processing and redundancy has been referred to in Chapter 2. To illustrate the advantages of the noncoherent optical system, we compare it to the coherent optical system.

3.1. PROPERTIES OF A COHERENT SYSTEM

A typical coherent system is shown in Figure 3.1. A point source of monochromatic light is placed in the front focal plane of a condenser. The object, which in this case *must* be a transparency, is placed in the emerging parallel light, and the imaging lens or lenses then collect the light emerging from the object. Typically the system first forms an image of the point source in the back focal plane of the imaging or transform lens. The presence of the object draws this image out into the Fraunhofer diffraction pattern of this object. This diffraction pattern then gives rise to the image further along the system.

The first thing to notice about this system is that the polar diagram of this effective source (pinhole and condenser) is *not* slowly varying. On the contrary, it peaks very strongly in an axial direction, with some 80% of the energy lying within a few seconds or a minute of the axis. It is not, therefore, possible to pick up essentially the same information in a number of directions around the axis. In fact, the whole diffraction pattern of the object must be collected to obtain complete information about it. Put another way, the object transmission function $A(x, y)$,

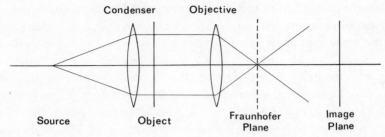

Figure 3.1 A typical coherent imaging system. Since all the light proceeds from a single point source, the information is carried only once through the system and noise accidentally introduced cannot be removed.

which in the case of coherent light is a complex amplitude transmission function, is itself the cause of light being diffracted out of the axial direction. Thus the local polar diagrams around $(x, y, 0)$ depend on $A(x, y)$ and are *not* independent of it. In other words, the whole concept of orthogonality in the pathway has broken down, except in so far as the original point source can be regarded as one of the two input functions. In geometrical optics this would remain orthogonal to the input function $A(x, y)$ because orthogonality is an essentially geometrical concept, but in wave optics the image of the point source is spoiled by diffraction at the input transparency. The geometrical case can be approximated to by allowing $\lambda \to 0$, when the Fraunhofer diffraction pattern steadily diminishes and becomes a point.

3.2. A SYSTEM WITHOUT REDUNDANCY

A very important property of the above coherent system is that it has no redundancy. There is only one point source, and once the information contained in the input transparency $A(x, y)$ has been imposed on the wavefront, it will propagate down the system. It cannot be totally removed by an averaging procedure designed to isolate information orthogonal to it.

The process of Gabor in line holography shows us first that the information in any subsequent plane is essentially the same, so that $A(x, y)$ may be recovered by holographic reconstruction. The exception is a special case where the diffraction pattern is recorded in or near the back focal plane of the objective, where the "reference beam" has become separated from the signal beams by being focused on the axis. Secondly, we know that any other transparency $B(x, y)$ superimposed on the system in a different plane is also recorded holographically. In principle it can also be recovered by holographic reconstruction, but only with the diffraction pattern of $A(x, y)$ indelibly superimposed on it. The two signals are, therefore, not fully separable. In particular, if $B(x, y)$ is, for example, a dusty surface in the optical system, the noise it produces becomes inseparable from the wanted signal. The worst case is a single black spot placed on axis in the back focal plane which produces a serious loss of energy and a serious disturbance of the image (dark field microscopy). The only way to guard against complete vulnerability to noise is to reintroduce redundancy, and this involves either abandoning coherence or modifying it considerably. It would be quite possible to *define* a coherent system in terms of an absence of redundancy.

3.3.   WHAT HAPPENS WHEN REDUNDANCY IS REINTRODUCED

Because the transition from a coherent, nonredundant system to a noncoherent system can proceed in stages, we gain considerable insight into the difference between the two systems.

First, imagine that the coherent optical system is provided with *two* point sources in the focal plane of the condenser (Figure 3.2). These sources yield two parallel beams emerging from the condenser at different angles. Two Fraunhofer diffraction patterns arise in the back focal plane of the main objective, but it is a characteristic of the imaging

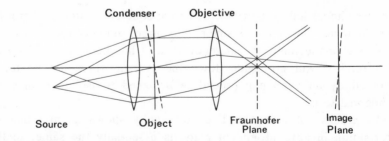

Figure 3.2   The effect of introducing a second point source is that the information is now carried *twice* through the system, and noise, therefore, plays a less important part than in a single point system. A fully noncoherent system has an indefinitely large number of source points and noise becomes negligible except in the object and image planes.

system that these two patterns join in the image plane to give a single image of twice the intensity. So far we have not said whether the two point sources are mutually coherent or mutually incoherent. If they are incoherent, there is absolutely no trouble and the intensities add at the image plane. We have also achieved an element of redundancy. A single black spot in the back focal plane can no longer block the image entirely; it can only halve its intensity because it can only obscure the image of one of the source points. As the number of mutually noncoherent source points is increased indefinitely, the system approaches the noncoherent systems of Chapter 2.

If, on the other hand, the two source points are mutually *coherent* the system behaves in a totally different manner. In the first instance, with two source points, the whole input pattern $A(x, y)$ has superimposed on it a set of Young interference fringes caused by the two coherent waves. These fringes are eliminated in the back focal plane of the main objective lens, owing to the separation of the source images, but they reappear in the image plane. This is a serious disturbance on top of the required signal.

As the number of coherently related source points is increased to N, a number of superimposed Young interference fringes appear in the object plane. In particular, there will be $\frac{1}{2}N(N-1)$ of them. As N increases indefinitely, one finds that this system of coherently related sources has reached a state of considerable confusion, which can only be described as a speckle pattern. An alternative way to achieve a speckle pattern is to place a piece of finely ground glass just in front of the condenser and illuminate from behind with a single point source. The ground glass screen smears the source over a finite area coherently thus giving a virtual source of many coherently related points.

3.4. THE EFFECT OF A DIFFUSER IN A COHERENT SYSTEM

We can describe the effect of a diffuser in a coherent system in a number of ways. In the first place we can take each image point or virtual image point in the front focal plane of the condenser in turn. In this way, each point gives rise to an individual Fraunhofer diffraction pattern in the back focal plane of the objective or imaging lens. Each such pattern is centered on a different point in the back focal plane, and each point is conjugate with its particular source point. We can imagine,

if the idea seems helpful, that the various source points emit photons in sequence, but that because of the coherent nature of the system the photons are phase related. Considered over an appreciable time we get a coherent convolution of the Fraunhofer pattern with the source pattern in the back focal plane.

A similar result is obtained by applying the convolution theorem to the diffuser and object. In object space we now have the product of the object and the diffuser. In Fourier space, (i.e., in the back focal plane) we have the convolution of the Fourier transform of the object, which is effectively its Fraunhofer pattern, and the Fourier transform of the diffusing screen, which is effectively the virtual source pattern in the front focal plane of the condenser.

The net result very greatly impedes the traditional methods of coherent image processing. These methods depend on placing a correcting filter in the Fourier or back focal plane of the system *so positioned* that its center lies on the axis at a point conjugate with the single source point. With a multiple source that emits photons in succession, it would be necessary to move the correcting filter around in the back focal plane so that its center was always conjugate with the particular point on the source that was emitting at that time. With a randomly triggered system of points this is not practicable. Redman has used a system in which a single point source is made to scan over the front focal plane of the condenser while the filter scans synchronously the back plane of the objective (Wolton and Redman 1972). This provides a very useful increase in redundancy.

The introduction of a diffuser into a coherent system can therefore increase redundancy at the expense of complicating any image processing. Certain speckle pattern techniques (Butters and Leendertz 1971) circumvent this problem, but they have low resolving power. Diffuser-induced redundancy (whether a transmitting diffuser or a diffusely reflecting surface on the object) is a very important factor in modern holography. The redundancy introduced can be very high, though there is always speckle noise which must be taken into account. Generally, such holograms are very successful when used for display purposes and not required to carry as much information as the holographic plate can carry. In a word they are heavily redundant.

So far we have used the word "redundant" in an intuitive sense, and the time has come to examine it more closely.

3.5. REDUNDANCY

The essential requirement for redundancy is that the object shall carry less information than the optical pathway is capable of handling. The upper limit to the information the pathway can handle is set by the wavelength of light and the geometry of the system. The latter is conveniently characterized by the Etendu of the system. This well-known quantity can be defined in a number of ways.

One way to define Etendu is to take the area of the object and multiply it by the solid angle subtended by the entrance pupil of the system as seen at the center of the object. An equivalent definition is to take the area of the entrance pupil and multiply it by the solid angle subtended by the object at the center of the pupil. Again, if A_1 is the area of the object, A_2 the area of the entrance pupil, and D is the distance between the two planes, the Etendu $E = A_1 A_2 / D^2$. It will be seen that Etendu has the dimensions of area.

It is well known that the number of independent optical channels in a given optical pathway is, to the small angle approximation, equal to E/λ^2 (see Appendix II). This represents the amount of information that the pathway can carry at any given instant of time. Time variation can, of course, be superimposed on the system, giving an overall bit-rate, but for purposes of comparison this simply multiplies everything by a constant factor.

We can now define redundancy as

$$R = \frac{\text{Information-carrying capacity of the pathway}}{\text{Information actually being carried}}$$

Consider, for example, a page from a printed book. Such an object seldom carries important information in excess of 8 cycles mm^{-1}. The text would be quite readable if reproduced by an optical system with a high frequency cut off at 8 cycles mm^{-1}. Even a halftone block seldom has more than 8 dots mm^{-1} in any direction and would be reproduced with some loss of contrast.

There is no difficulty at all in photoreducing the page of such a book with a resolving power of 30 lines mm^{-1}. All that is required is a lens with a relative aperture of 1/60 in object space and for a 5:1 reduction this involves a lens working at $F/10$. Such a copying system is quite common.

In this case, we can calculate the redundancy simply in terms of the squares of the spatial frequencies involved

$$R = \frac{(30)^2}{(8)^2} = 14$$

Thus if one of the 14 possible channels is blocked (e.g., by dirt on the imaging lens), then the loss of contrast is 7%, which is normally quite unimportant.

Systems used in noncoherent data processing frequently have much higher degrees of redundancy than described in the above example. For instance, a noncoherent optical correlator will frequently have a lens working at $F/3$. The data planes are nearer than in the case of a $5:1$ photographic reduction, and, in any case, the rate of input on the data planes is not normally high. It must be remembered that noncoherent systems are essentially geometrical in operation and that diffraction must be eliminated. Even in short systems this limits practical input frequencies to 1 or 2 cycles mm^{-1}, although fairly large input areas can be tolerated. There is no real difficulty in putting in 1000 data points; however, there may be some difficulty in processing the output data with sufficient precision to make all the input points significant.

Thus in a noncoherent correlator or a Fourier transformer, we may have an input plane in the front focal plane of the lens, where an $F/3$ lens can in principle resolve 500 lines mm^{-1}. If the input frequencies do not exceed 2 lines mm^{-1} we have $R = (250)^2 = 62,500$. Part of this redundancy can be used to swamp aberrations in the lens and part is available to permit parallel processing.

3.6. PARALLEL PROCESSING

There is always a trade-off between redundancy and parallel processing. The concept of parallel processing implies that the overall optical pathway is subdivided into sections, each of which is dedicated to a particular processing function. The redundancy within each subsection is then the information-carrying capacity of that subsection divided by the total input information. As long as the quotient is greater than one the operation is theoretically possible.

Returning to the Fourier transformer, imagine we have 1000 input points (roughly 32×32 squares). We can now expect observations at not more than 1000 output points, or we have insufficient input data to specify the outputs. Each subsection of the system must occupy 1/1000 of the pathway, and the redundancy per subsection falls to 62.5. This is still a very respectable redundancy and the system works very well within these limits. Thus, noncoherent systems tend to have moderate data-handling capacity and repay this with improved redundancy.

The complementary concepts of redundancy and parallel processing can therefore be used in designing an effective noncoherent optical processing system.

3.7. ADVANTAGES OF A NONCOHERENT DATA PROCESSING SYSTEM

The main advantages of a noncoherent system are a combination of redundancy and parallel processing and a very high resistance to noise. The total information handling capacity of the system falls below that theoretically possible with a coherent system, but it must be remembered that the optics of a coherent system must be carefully designed to push the system to the theoretical limit. In noncoherent systems one tends to use larger aperture lenses in order to increase the theoretical redundancy of the system, and one relies on a reserve of redundancy to overcome aberrations in the system. We have, for example, built two models of the Fourier transformer, one with a well-corrected photographic objective and the other with a simple doublet telescope lens of similar aperture and focal length. Although the performance of the two instruments is not obviously different, a careful examination of the performance at the edge of the field reveals better contrast from the photographic objective.

REFERENCES

Butters, J. N. and J. A. Leendertz (1971). *Opt. Laser Tech.* **3**, 26–30.
Wolton, W. P. and J. D. Redman (1972). *Report of 10th International Congress on High Speed Photography, Nice*, John Wiley & Sons, London.

4

Transparent Processing
Masks and Their Use

Transparent processing masks are conveniently made photographically. They are made to represent the input function as a variation in intensity rather than a variation in amplitude as used in coherent optical processing. In this system, it is also necessary to introduce DC bias into the function in order to avoid negative values of intensity.

Using a computer graph plotter with a gray scale output is by far the simplest way to generate an input function. Some of these devices work by photographing a cathode ray tube display, in which case a photographic transparency is immediately available.The transparency may not be at the correct scale, in which case the display has to be rephotographed. No photographic process is exactly linear, so that it is a wise precaution to make the graph plotter produce a marginal step wedge on the wanted pattern. This consists of a series of areas whose intensities bear a constant ratio to one another, say $\sqrt{2}$. The corresponding areas in the final photograph can then be examined by a densitometer to check the overall linearity of the process. If it is found to be seriously nonlinear, the computer can be reprogrammed to produce an output that corrects for the measured nonlinearities in the photographic process. Needless to say, the exposure and development of the photographic procedure must be carefully standardized if the photograph is to be reproducible. It is advisable to ensure that adequate stocks of materials are available, because the procedure must be recalibrated if the batch number of the photographic materials is changed. Provided precautions are taken comparable with those currently employed for color photography, there is no difficulty in producing results which repeat within 5%.

In some cases, where intensity variation in one direction will suffice, use may be made of the cylindrical lens technique described in Chapter 1. Sprague and Thompson (1972) have also used a mask that automatically corrects for the nonlinearities of the photographic process.

4.1. THE COMBINATION OF TRANSPARENT MASKS

As indicated in Chapter 2, it is very useful to combine two transparent input masks. With certain adjustments, the optical processor can be made to give either a convolution or a correlation of the two input functions. This in turn can be used to perform various calculations, such as extracting a single Fourier coefficient by correlating the general input with a sine wave representing the desired frequency.

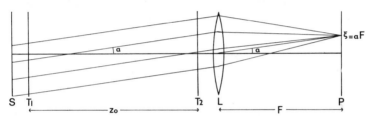

Figure 4.1 A single optical processor using a bundle of parallel beams. Diffuse source = S, first input = T_1, second input = T_2, integrating lens = L, output screen or plate = P.

A simple optical processor is shown in Figure 4.1. It consists of a diffuse source, followed by two transparencies, a lens, and a screen or plate. The two transparencies are ideally separated by a distance that is large compared with their lateral extent. The screen or plate should be in the back focal plane of the lens. It can be shown that the output pattern on the screen or plate is a correlation between the two input patterns.

In order to see this, it is necessary to examine carefully the action of the lens and plate. Since, in this application, the photographic plate is placed in the focal plane of the lens, all rays with direction cosines l and m that form angles with the axis of α, β are focused to a single point in the back focal plane of the lens (i.e., to a single point on the photographic plate). The luminous flux associated with each little bundle of rays is added together during the focusing process, the point being that the various bundles striking the lens at different places on its front surface fall on the plate from different directions. Since the plate is sensitive to light from any direction, the effect at the focused point is to integrate over direction. In the space in front of the lens we are, therefore, integrating for a fixed (α, β) or (l, m) over the entrance pupil of the lens. In many expositions of this subject the lens is said to be used as an integrator. More strictly it is the lens plate combination that does the integration, because of the directional integration at the plate. A Lambertian diffusing screen placed in the same position as the plate will also integrate over direction, at least within the cone of an ordinary lens. In practice, diffusing screens are often used that do not so fully diffuse the light, but pass a greater fraction of the incident energy. In this case, the effective scatter cone of the diffuser should be matched with the angular cone of the lens, that is, to its F/number.

Suppose the transparency in the first plane is represented by $T_1(x, y)$; that is, a ray of unit intensity falling on the transparency from the source emerges with an intensity $T_1(x, y)$ from the point (x, y). Similarly, the transparency in the second plane is represented by $T_2(x, y)$. If the planes are a distance z_0 apart, and we consider a ray passing through (x, y) in the plane of T_1, with direction cosines l and m, the ray will pass through T_2 at the point $(x + lz_0, y + mz_0)$ and its final intensity will be

$$T_1(x, y) \cdot T_2(x + lz_0, y + mz_0)$$

If we now use the integrating effect of the lens and plate over the x, y region, we see that the total intensity reaching a point (lF, mF) in the back focal plane of the lens (focal length F) will be

$$I(l, m) = \iint T_1(x, y) \cdot T_2(x + lz_0, y + mz_0) \, dx \, dy$$

the integration being over the clear areas of T_1 and T_2. This is the correlation coefficient of T_1 and T_2 with offset (lz_0, mz_0). If we now regard l and m as variables, $I(l, m)$ becomes the correlation function of T_1 and T_2 with scale z_0.

The convolution of T_1 and T_2 will be obtained if either T_1 or T_2 is inverted; for example, by using $T_2'(x, y) = T_2(-x, -y)$. The direction cosines l and m may also be related to linear coordinates $\xi = lF$, $\eta = mF$ in the back focal plane.

Notice that this system evaluates all points in $I(l, m)$ simultaneously; that is, it is a case of a parallel processor. In principle it is without redundancy but the implicit assumption of the geometrical optics used in its derivation means that because neither T_1 nor T_2 can contain details of wavelength or diffraction proportions redundancy is still present. The existence of a blemish occupying 1% of the area of either transparency will produce a scarcely noticeable effect on $I(l, m)$ whereas such a blemish in a coherent correlator would produce most noticeable diffraction effects.

4.2. THE CORRELATOR WITH NEGATIVE INPUTS: THE EFFECT OF DC BIAS

To handle functions with negative numbers, we resort to the method of DC bias. If $T_1(x, y)$ and $T_2(x, y)$ contain negative numbers and require the addition of DC bias terms of magnitude A and B we now have

$$
\begin{aligned}
\text{Integral} &= \iint [A + T_1(x, y)] \cdot [B + T_2(x + lz_0, y + mz_0)] \, dx \, dy \\
&= AB \iint dx \, dy + B \iint T_1(x, y) \, dx \, dy \\
&\quad + A \iint T_2(x + lz_0, y + mz_0) \, dx \, dy + I(l, m)
\end{aligned}
$$

The output, therefore, consists of the required correlation function $I(l, m)$, together with three extra terms. The first two terms are independent of l and m and represent a DC bias in the output plane. The third term is very similar in form to the second, except that the origin of coordinates has been shifted to $(-lz_0, -mz_0)$. Correlation integrals are theoretically of infinite extent; in practice, they are evaluated over finite ranges depending on the sizes of T_1 and T_2. The shift in the origin must, therefore, be accompanied by a corresponding shift in the limits of integration so that the third term is also constant. We see then that the effect of using DC bias terms in T_1 and T_2 is to introduce a considerable DC bias term into the output. Since this term may well be much greater than that necessary to ensure that $I(l, m)$ is always positive, there is a considerable loss of contrast.

4.3. THE PROJECTIVE VARIATION

The use of a lens can be avoided by a simple variation, in which the scale of $T_2(x, y)$ is reduced. Expressing this in its simplest term, suppose the scale of $T_2(x, y)$ is half the scale of $T_1(x, y)$. Place $T_1(x, y)$ in the plane $z = 0$; T_2 in the plane $z = z_0$; and the photographic plate in the plane $z = 2z_0$ (Figure 4.2). Then the ray that originally moved parallel to the axis in Figure 4.1, and was focused by the lens on axis, is now seen to move from the point (x, y) in T_1 to the corresponding point in T_2, which, because of the reduced scale, is now $(x/2, y/2)$. It thus crosses the axis in the plane of the plate.

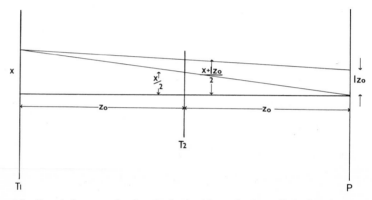

Figure 4.2 Correlation can also be obtained without the lens, if the input T_2 is smaller than the input T_1, giving a point of convergence at which point the screen or plate P must be placed.

Similarly, the ray that had direction cosines l and m in Figure 4.1 now moves from (x, y) in T_1 to the point corresponding to $(x + lz_0, y + mz_0)$ in T_2, which is situated at the point $[(x + lz_0)/2, (y + mz_0)/2]$. Applying similar triangles to this case we find that the x coordinate of the line is reduced from x to $(x + lz_0)/2$ in a distance z_0 and is reduced by twice this amount in the distance $2z_0$. We thus find it cuts the plane $2z_0$ at the point whose x coordinate is

$$x - 2\left\{x - \frac{x + lz_0}{2}\right\} = lz_0$$

Similarly, its y coordinate is mz_0. It will be noted that this point is independent of the position of (x, y) so that *all* lines that in Figure 4.1

had direction cosines l and m are transformed in Figure 4.2 into lines passing through (lz_0, mz_0) in the plane $z = 2z_0$. The photographic plate integrates the effect over all angles, as before, and the correlation between T_1 and T_2 is produced in the plane P.

The use of the projective arrangement requires the complication of producing correctly scaled transparencies T_1 and T_2. On the other hand, it removes the need for the lens and problems associated with lens aberrations. Both schemes have been extensively used, each having its particular advantages.

4.4. APPLICATIONS OF THE NONCOHERENT CORRELATOR

Early applications of the noncoherent correlator were noted in Chapter 1 when Robertson (1943) and Haag (1944) used correlators of this type to work out Patterson projections in X-ray crystallography. It is not known whether the correlators were extensively used, but they were certainly used in the laboratories of origin.

McLachlan (1962) has also described optical correlators that have a variety of purposes. The most complicated correlator described is used for optical character recognition. The technique of correlating the input characters with all the characters of the alphabet, either in parallel or successively, is very ingenious, but it is clumsy compared with methods now available.

Silva and Rogers (1975) have also described the use of a noncoherent optical correlator in conjunction with a technique derived by Mertz and Young (1961) and Young (1963). This consists of using the shadow of a zone plate, cast by a star field, as a noncoherent "hologram" of the input pattern. Using a lens type correlator, Silva and Rogers have shown that the composite zone plate shadow has only to be correlated noncoherently with a sharp zone plate drawn on the same scale to recover the shadowing input pattern.

4.5. A SPECIAL CASE: THE SPATIAL FREQUENCY FILTER

Although only general correlators are mentioned above, in the sense that T_1 and T_2 may be chosen to represent any functions, a particular case of importance is when T_2 represents a sinusoidal wave or a sufficiently close approximation to it. In this case, we derive a cross-correlation function, the principal term of which is the corresponding Fourier coefficient of the equivalent frequency in T_1. By using a sufficient number of correlations in parallel, a series of Fourier coefficient can be derived simultaneously.

It is not possible to construct a sinusoidal intensity transmission mask, because negative values are inadmissible. The best approximation possible for $T_2(x, y)$ is

$$T_2(x, y) = \tfrac{1}{2}\{1 + \cos(\alpha x + \beta y)\}$$

a sinusoidal variation of intensity transmission at an angle making intercepts of α and β on the x and y axes, respectively.

The correlation between $T_1(x, y)$ and this value of T_2 is

$$C_{\alpha\beta}(p, q) = \iint T_1(x, y)\tfrac{1}{2}\{1 + \cos[\alpha(x + p) + \beta(y + q)]\}\, dx\, dy$$

The value of this expression at the center of the correlation plane (on the axis) where $p = q = 0$ is

$$C_{\alpha\beta}(0, 0) = \iint T_1(x, y) \cdot \tfrac{1}{2}\{1 + \cos(\alpha x + \beta y)\}\, dx\, dy$$

This divides into two terms

$$\tfrac{1}{2}\iint T_1(x, y)\, dx\, dy$$

which gives the integrated transmission of $T_1(x, y)$, which is a DC bias term, and

$$\tfrac{1}{2}\iint T_1(x, y) \cos(\alpha y + \beta y)\, dx\, dy$$

which is the Fourier coefficient of the period $\cos(\alpha x + \beta y)$ in $T_1(x, y)$.

If we look further at $C_{\alpha\beta}(p, q)$, we see that if p is increased from 0 to $2\pi/\alpha$ or q from 0 to $2\pi/\beta$, the value of the cosine term remains unaltered. It follows that $C_{\alpha\beta}(p, q)$ in the correlation plane is a periodic function, with a period corresponding to the analysis wave. Motion in the pq plane is equivalent to shifting the phase of the $\cos(\alpha x + \beta y)$ term and we can, for instance, convert it into a sine term. Of practical importance is that the amplitude and phase of the periodic or AC signal is equivalent to the amplitude and phase of the coefficient (α, β) in the

Fourier transform of $T_1(x, y)$. This can be measured relative to the DC bias by methods involving photodetectors that feed into electronic measuring circuits.

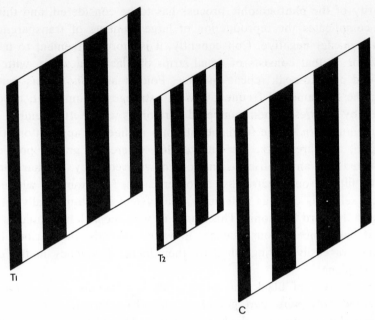

Figure 4.3 The spatial frequency filter. The input T_1 interacts with the analyzing grid T_2 to give a sharp shadow on the correlating plane C.

For student demonstration, a simple projective system can be set up with a variable spacing between the input $T_1(x, y)$ and the analysis grid $T_2(x, y)$ working onto a screen. The scale of $T_2(x, y)$ must be smaller than the highest frequency (shortest spacing) to be analyzed in $T_1(x, y)$, but subject to this, a range of frequencies can be brought into "tune" by altering the spacing between T_1 and T_2. The contrast of the correlogram (shadow) can be judged by eye and brought to a maximum. The relevant frequency in T_1 can then be calculated from the known frequency in T_2 and the projective magnification of the system (Figure 4.3).

For character recognition the correlation again is most conveniently done in the projective system, which lends itself to building up a battery of parallel processors. By placing the sinusoidal grating in the position T_2, we can use a printed sheet of paper as the input T_1. It is therefore applicable to character recognition from printed material. In principle, of course, the sinusoidal input could be at T_1 and the unknown at T_2, but this makes parallel processing difficult and the use of a paper input impossible.

The construction of a sinusoidal input function is a little difficult, even using the cylindrical lens technique from a cutout wave. The non-linearity of the photographic process has to be considered, and this in turn complicates the reproduction of large numbers of transparencies from a master negative. Consequently, it is more convenient to use a mask for T_2 that consists of equal strips of black and white, with the required peak-to-peak repeat distance. Fourier analysis of this grating gives the fundamental frequency as the strongest component, accompanied by a series of odd-numbered harmonics whose nth member has an amplitude $1/n$ of the fundamental. In a number of applications (i.e., O. T. F. measurements; see Chapter 10), where the grating profile is converted into an electrical signal of known frequency, the harmonics can be filtered out electrically. In other cases, for example, where an optical selsyn is used as a detector, the system is automatically insensitive to the third harmonic. This leaves us with the fifth harmonic as the lowest harmonic of consequence. In visual systems, the various harmonics are easily distinguished by their higher frequency in the correlation plane.

Reproduction of black and white grids is relatively easy as one is concerned only with two points on the characteristic curve of the photographic emulsion: black and white. The shape of the curve between these two points is unimportant, provided the gradation is steep enough. Emulsions with very steep characteristics are widely used for halftone and line reproduction, where they have a digitizing function very similar to a Schmidt trigger in electronics.

A grid structure of this kind, placed a certain distance from a diffusing screen, constitutes a spatial frequency filter for any object placed a given distance from it. That is to say it passes only a fixed frequency. A similar effect occurs if the diffuse screen is replaced by a black and white grid of the same spacing as the "in tune" image.

A delta function input will, of course, cast a well-defined shadow for all frequencies because it transforms into a white spectrum.

4.6. REDUNDANCY IN THE SPATIAL FREQUENCY FILTER

Since the spatial frequency filter isolates just one spatial frequency from the whole field, it is heavily redundant. There is the obvious strong redundancy that arises from the fact that blurring in the direction of the lines on T_2 is always possible without loss of information. There is the further redundancy of the periodic output that repeats the value of $C_{\alpha\beta}(0,0)$ at intervals $2\pi/\alpha$ and $2\pi/\beta$ in the p and q directions. Consequently, the signal-to-noise ratio is very good.

The use of the spatial frequency filter in character recognition is described by Leifer, Rogers, and Stephens (1969) and in Chapter 10 of this book.

REFERENCES

Haag, G. (1944). *Nature (GB)* **153**, 81.

Leifer, I., G. L. Rogers, and N. W. F. Stephens (1969). *Opt. Acta* **16**, 535.

McLachlan, D. (1962). *J. Opt. Soc. Amer.* **52**, 454.

Mertz, L. and N. A. Young (1961). *Proceedings of the I.C.O. Conference on Optical Instrumentation*, London, 305.

Robertson, J. M. (1943). *Nature (GB)* **152**, 411.

Silva, R. and Gordon L. Rogers (1975). *J. Opt. Soc. Amer.* **65**, 1448–50.

Sprague, R. A. and B. J. Thompson (1972). *Appl. Opt.* **11**, 1469.

Young, N. O. (1963). *Sky Telesc.* **25**, 8–9.

5

Noncoherent
Fourier Transformation

In his book, *Transformations in Optics*, Lawrence Mertz (1965) described a method of Fourier transformation involving three zone plates, which yielded a very low-contrast output because the third zone plate was unnecessary and merely reduced the contrast. Such an output is not unusual in noncoherent data processing, but unfortunately, Mertz did not follow up the idea.

Richardson (1972) has described in a patent a system of Fourier transformation using two zone plates. The mathematics of the method is developed in great detail and we await further publications on its use.

5.1. THREE-MASK COMPUTING SYSTEMS

Two input computing systems can be treated by the method of orthogonality as developed by Dorrestein (1950). Three mask systems cannot be so treated, since it is not possible to find three mutually orthogonal planes in an optical system. Each arrangement must, therefore be treated on its own merit.

In some cases, two of the masks are designed to produce a particular effect in the plane of the third mask. In the Fourier transformer (Stephens and Rogers 1974), two zone plates are arranged, one either side of the input mask, so they generate a set of moire fringes across the mask when viewed from an off-axis position. This is equivalent to multiplying the input mask with a cosine function. Integration over the

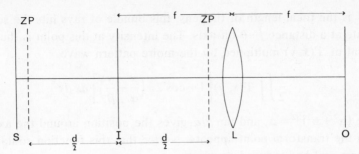

Figure 5.1 The Fourier transformer. Two zone plates are illuminated from a source S on the left and the input function I is placed halfway between them. An integrating lens L is so arranged that the input function is in its front focal plane, and the output screen O is in its back focal plane. This ensures orthogonality between input and output.

field with a lens-plate combination then gives the cosine Fourier coefficient for that particular frequency.

The general configuration is shown in Figure 5.1. By arranging the input mask in the front focal plane of the lens and the plate or diffusing screen in the back focal plane, we at least ensure that the input and output start orthogonal. The two zone plates are then arranged equidistant from the input mask. The scale of the zone plates is chosen to be large enough to make any diffraction effects negligible. The effect is the purely geometrical one associated with the moire pattern between the two zone plates (Oster, Wasserman, and Zwerling 1964).

If two zone plates of the same basic radius r_1 are placed in contact, linear moire fringes are obtained. The spacing of these fringes are inversely related to the distance between centers of the zone plates, and they lie along a direction perpendicular to the join of the two centers.

When the zone plates are *not* in contact, the effective distance between the centers depends on the angular offset of the viewing direction. Thus if the distance between the planes of the zone plates is d as in Figure 5.1 and we consider a bundle of parallel rays crossing the axis at a small angle θ, the effective offset of the centers is $\theta \cdot d$. Substituting this in the fringe spacing equation of Oster, Wasserman, and Zwerling (1964), we get a spacing Δ

$$\Delta = \frac{r_1^2}{\theta d}$$

r_1 being the innermost radius of the zone plates.

If f is the focal length of the lens, this bundle of rays hits the screen or plate at a distance $f \cdot \theta$ off axis. The intensity at this point is thus the integral of $T(x, y)$ multiplied by the moire pattern wave

$$\frac{1}{2} \iint T(x, y) \left[1 + \cos 2\pi \left(\frac{x}{\alpha} + \frac{y}{\beta} \right) \right] dx \, dy$$

where $(\alpha^2 + \beta^2)^{1/2} = \Delta$, and $\tan \beta/\alpha$ gives the position around the axis at which the transform point appears. Notice that this function contains a DC term and has reduced contrast.

5.2. PROPERTIES OF THE COSINE TRANSFORM

The cosine transform is a complete solution to the transform of $T(x, y)$ only if the function $T(x, y)$ is centrosymmetrical and, therefore, expressible as a sum of cosines. If the function $T(x, y)$ is displaced sideways, the transform alters. In particular, if $T(x, y)$ is a regularly repeated pattern that is centrosymmetrical, it will give rise to peaks in the transform plane corresponding to the spectra from the equivalent grating in coherent light. If, however, $T(x, y)$ is moved half a period sideways, the peaks change into corresponding troughs, and one gets black shadows rather than brighter dots. This is of considerable interest in educating students. Because the Fraunhofer (coherent) apparatus is insensitive to phase changes, they cannot be observed. However, the noncoherent Fourier transformer using zone plates enables the effects of lateral shifts to be demonstrated. With an apparatus of reasonable size, it is also very easy to choose parameters to give a much bigger transform pattern than is possible with Fraunhofer diffraction. One can even postulate a fictitious "equivalent wavelength" which is commonly 0.1–1 mm.

5.3. THE COMPLETE FOURIER TRANSFORM: SINE AND COSINE TRANSFORMERS

The complete transform of $T(x, y)$ can be calculated if we can obtain sine and cosine transforms independently. This we can do by generating a moire pattern with a phase shift.

Walls and Southworth (1975) have shown that if a zone plate forms a moire pattern with a linear grid, the result is two other zone plates, but these have a variable "phase." They expand and contract as the linear system is passed across the original zone plate in the same way a set of Fabry Perot fringes will, when the plate separation is slowly altered. On the other hand, if we were to take two zone plates of unequal phase we could generate a linear moire pattern that is not symmetrically related to either. We can in particular produce a "sine" set of fringes by using two different zone plates in our apparatus where the radii obey the relations

$$\text{I} \qquad r_n = r \cdot n^{1/2} \qquad\qquad \text{cosine}$$

$$\text{II} \qquad r_n = r(n - \tfrac{1}{2})^{1/2} \qquad \text{sine}$$

where r is the radius of the first Fresnel half period. These are cosine and sine zone plates, respectively. Two sine zone plates will, of course, produce cosine fringes; but a cosine and a sine zone plate produce sine fringes.

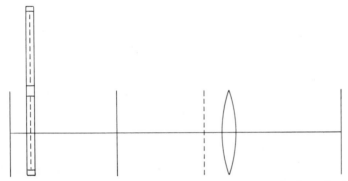

Figure 5.2   The sine/cosine transformer, with a slide allowing transfer from sine to cosine arrangement.

The technique is thus to recover the transform of $T(x, y)$ using two similar zone plates and then again with one zone plate of each type. The resulting patterns give the real and imaginary parts of the complete transform of $T(x, y)$. Various ways of doing this have been explored. The simplest method is to have a slide, carrying one sine and one cosine zone plate side by side (Figure 5.2). The slide is moved across the apparatus and is provided with stops so that either a sine or a cosine zone plate can be put on axis. The second zone plate, further down the apparatus, is kept constant.

An attempt has been made to combine sine and cosine zone plates into one mask by using dye-coupling developers to produce the sine and cosine images in different colors. The color contrast resulting is, however, too weak to be useful.

5.4.   THE FREQUENCY RANGE OF THE SYSTEM

There is an absolute upper limit to the frequency range of the system set by vignetting at the edges of the zone plates. The plates are necessarily of finite size; let us suppose they have a diameter D. Then two zone plates separated by a distance d will only pass light up to an off-axis angle θ given by

$$\tan \theta = \frac{D}{d} = \frac{\xi_{max}}{f}$$

where ξ_{max} is the radius of the region of the screen or plate illuminated with a lens of focal length f (see Figure 5.3). The maximum frequency S_{max} in the plane of the moire fringes is given by

$$S_{max} = \frac{1}{\Delta_{min}} = \frac{\theta_{max} d}{r_1^2}$$

For small angles we can write $\theta_{max} = D/d$

$$\frac{1}{\Delta_{min}} = \frac{D}{r_1^2}$$

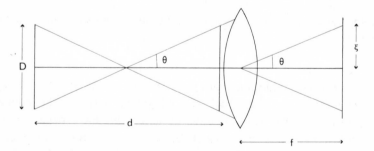

Figure 5.3 Diagram to illustrate vignetting and finite frequency range in the Fourier transformer. D = diameter of operative zone plates, d = their separation, f = the focal length of the integrating lens, and ξ = the off-axis distance corresponding to an oblique bundle at angle θ.

Now if n is the number of half-period zones in the zone plate, $D = 2r_n = 2r_1 \cdot n^{1/2}$, so that

$$S_{max} = \frac{1}{\Delta_{min}} = \frac{2 \cdot n^{1/2}}{r_1}$$

We see that the maximum frequency possible with the instrument depends only on the radius of the first half-period zone and the number of zones. In particular, the separation d falls out of the equation. The separation does, however, affect θ_{max} and ξ_{max}, and should be large enough not to call for a lens with a wide angular field.

A similar result arises if we equate Δ_{min} to the spacing of the outside zones; vignetting is complete at this value. Light falls off severely from 60% of this value up to the theoretical limit. At 40% of this offset, that is, at Freq $= 0.8n^{1/2}/r_1$, the light has already fallen to roughly 50% of its central value, while at $1.2n^{1/2}/r_1$ it is less than 30%. If we accept the 50% level as appropriate to vignetting, as is usual in defining the extent of an optical field, we see the maximum frequency is $0.8n^{1/2}/r_1$.

The system has a lower frequency limit. If we consider the situation where $\Delta = 2D$ we see the fringe width is twice the diameter of either zone plate. In practice, this means that the field is very nearly uniform, either light or dark according to the phase. In fact, the condition $\Delta \simeq D$ is very close to the condition for the Airy disk in coherent optics (strictly $1.22\Delta = D$) since the Airy disk reaches its minimum when there are 1.22 fringes across the telescope objective. There is thus always a bright central spot with a dark rim when the mask $T(x, y)$ is absent, and this represents the lowest frequency the apparatus can detect.

An important parameter of the system is the ratio of the maximum to minimum determinable frequencies. It is convenient to refer this ratio to the plate or film where the parameter ξ represents the distance off axis. We assume θ is small, giving

$$\xi_{max} = f\theta_{max} = \frac{Df}{d} = \frac{2n^{1/2}r_1 f}{d}$$

also

$$\xi_{min} = f\theta_{min} = \frac{1.22r_1^2}{Dd} f = \frac{1.22r_1 f}{2n^{1/2} \cdot d}$$

$$= \frac{0.61r_1 f}{n^{1/2}d}$$

we get $\xi_{max}/\xi_{min} = 2/0.61n = 3.28n$.

A more realistic figure uses the value of ξ to 50% viz

$$\xi_{50} = \frac{1.6 n^{1/2} r_1 f}{d}$$

giving that $\xi_{50}/\xi_{min} = 0.8/0.61 n = 1.31 n$. Not unexpectedly this ratio turns out to be dependent only on the number of zones on the two zone plates.

A further complication is that the process of moire fringe generation is not completely unambiguous. It is well known (Rogers 1959, 1977; Leifer, Walls, and Southworth 1973) that two grids will generate two different moire patterns corresponding to sum and difference vectors in frequency space. If the grids have a harmonic content, further patterns are generated but we shall ignore them here.

The changeover from one form to the other occurs when the characteristic frequencies interchange; the pattern with the lowest spatial frequency is always the most conspicuous. For a small separation of the zone plate centers, the linear fringes are by far the most important. As the separation increases and becomes comparable with the zone plate radius, a moire pattern that resembles a zone plate appears halfway between the centers of the generating grids. This is the sum pattern and has low frequencies near the axis.

The changeover cannot be calculated theoretically without many assumptions, but a practical test based on visual judgment suggests that the zone-plate-like moire fringe system is unimportant for separations below the 50% cutoff mark. This criterion is, therefore, preferred and will be used hereafter.

Richardson (1972) was very concerned with this effect, but by limiting the field to the 50% cutoff point one can get satisfactory results.

5.5. REDUNDANCY IN A THREE-MASK SYSTEM

Once again the redundancy of the system is theoretically zero, because each value of θ corresponds to a different point in the transform. The requirement that the system is nowhere carrying detail fine enough to produce diffraction effects limits the range of input frequencies. Thus the amount of input information used under these conditions is small enough for redundancy to occur.

The simplest approach to redundancy is to compare the value of ξ_{min}

calculated above by using the analogy with an "Airy disk" with the actual Airy disk of the objective using the mean wavelength of the experiment, which is the classical measure of diffraction limitation.

The objective has a focal length f and its diameter must be at least as large as the zone plates with which it is used. This gives for the radius of its Airy disk

$$\xi = \frac{1.22\lambda f}{D}$$

To be compared with

$$\xi = \frac{1.22 r_1 f}{2n^{1/2} d}$$

for the noncoherent system. The potential information-carrying capacity of the system/actual used capacity depends on the square of this ratio. The ratio is thus

$$\frac{r_1}{2n^{1/2} d} \cdot \frac{D}{\lambda}$$

But $D = 2n^{1/2} \cdot r_1$ giving $r_1^2/d\lambda$. But $r_1^2/\lambda = F$, the coherent focal length of zone plates used, which we have assumed is $\gg d$ to avoid diffraction.

The redundancy is therefore $(F/d)^2$, and depends on the ratio of the coherent focal length of the zone plates to their separation. The system necessarily has a high degree of redundancy.

It is interesting to note that Stephens and Rogers (1974) used the concept of a "notional" wavelength for the transformer, viewed as an analogue of a Fraunhofer apparatus. This "notional" focal length is such that the focal length of the zone plates for this fictitious wavelength is d.

We have discussed this particular system in detail, partly because a special study is required for any three-mask system, but also because it reveals important features of noncoherent optical processing systems. In particular, we see that these systems have high redundancy, and this is a direct consequence of their use in the geometrical optics region. As against this, the effective information-carrying capacity of the channel is correspondingly reduced. The noncoherent system thus offers us a controllable trade-off between information-carrying capacity and redundancy, which the ordinary coherent system does not offer.

REFERENCES

Dorrestein, R. (1950). *Philips Res. Rep.* **5**, 116.

Leifer, I., J. M. Walls, and H. N. Southworth (1973), *Opt. Acta* **20**, 33.

Mertz, L. (1965). *Transformations in Optics*, John Wiley & Sons, New York, pp. 94–95.

Oster, G., M. Wasserman, and C. Zwerling (1964). *J. Opt. Soc. Amer.* **54**, 169.

Richardson, J. M. (1972). U.S. Patent 3,669,528.

Rogers, G. L. (1959). *Proc. Phys. Soc.* (Eng.) **73**, 142.

Rogers, G. L. (1977). *Opt. Acta* **24**, 1–13.

Stephens, N. W. F. and G. L. Rogers, (1974). *Phys. Educ.* (*GB*) **9**, 331.

Walls, J. M. and H. N. Southworth (1975). *Opt. Acta* **22**, 591.

6

The DC Bias

The problem of DC bias in noncoherent optical data processing will be evident by now. There are a limited number of ways to mitigate this effect directly, and a much wider choice of methods using optical modulation. The latter is the subject of the next two chapters.

6.1. AMPLIFICATION AND CUTTING

The output of an optical data processing system is normally a two-dimensional field with a limited range of intensities from I_1 to I_2. The ratio of the difference $I_2 - I_1$ over either I_2 or, preferably, $I_1 + I_2$ can be taken as a measure of the contrast range of the output. The main problem is that this contrast range is often very small, say 5%. Such contrasts can be detected by the human eye, but only with great difficulty. Small variations within this range get lost altogether.

It is not sufficient simply to amplify intensities uniformly over the field, because this does not affect the ratio $(I_2 - I_1)/(I_2 + I_1)$. Amplification can be obtained by using a closed-circuit television link. In this case, we have two electronic controls at our disposal, "brightness" and "contrast." Using only maximum contrast simply gives a picture of unacceptable overall brightness. The brightness control must also be turned down to bring the output from I_1 to a level just above black. This is cutting the range of the output signal. The contrast control should then be set to bring I_2 up toward the maximum acceptable brightness. In many sets, these two controls are not fully independent, and a successive adjustment may be necessary to achieve the desired results. It

45

may also happen that the amplification at maximum contrast is insufficient, and it may be desirable to introduce an additional stage of amplification.

The use of a closed-circuit television link of adequate gain can substantially improve a noncoherent processing system, and is always worth trying. The most likely source of difficulty is vignetting in the optical system. This arises from off-axis pencils carrying less illumination than axial pencils. Some effect of this kind is inevitable with two-mask systems of finite lateral extent, since the edges of the masks produce a differential cutoff for oblique beams. The only situation where this does not apply is when the masks are largely opaque, save for a cluster of holes close to the center of the systems in each mask. It is then reasonably easy to ensure that the entrance pupil of the following lens is large enough to collect all the light passing.

The consequence of vignetting is that one can no longer set I_1 just above the black level all over the field. If it is set correctly in the center, it is below the black level at the edge, whereas if set for the edge it is too bright in the center. The latter is preferable, since no information is lost, but the usable scale is nevertheless compressed. The ideal is to design to minimize or avoid vignetting, but in some devices such as the Fourier transformer this is very difficult. The best that can be done is to impose a limit on the output field at an acceptable degree of fall off.

6.2. PHOTOGRAPHIC CONTROL

A similar type of control can be applied when using a photographic recording process. The system is not as flexible as a television link and the results are not available in real time. The photographic system depends essentially on the nonlinear properties of the photographic plate or film. This in turn depends on the type of emulsion used.

To increase the contrast of the output, we will use a high-contrast film. Fortunately, high-contrast films show a type of nonlinearity suited to this purpose; that is, they have a relatively sharp cutoff at low intensities. It is customary to represent the performance of a film by plotting the density of the processed film against the logarithm (to base 10) of the exposure needed to produce it. A standard processing procedure is specified in advance.

A typical curve for a high-contrast film is shown in Figure 6.1. At low

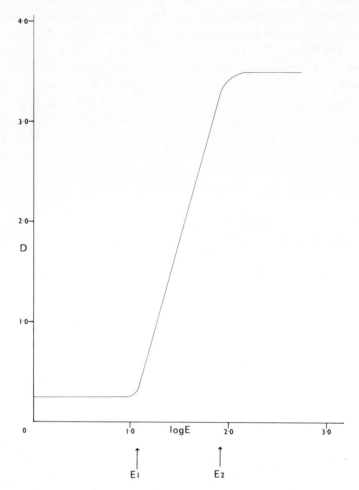

Figure 6.1   The characteristic curve of a high-contrast emulsion. The emulsion gives a high-contrast image for a range of exposures from E_1 to E_2. If the DC bias can be arranged so that the greatest negative number gives an exposure E_1 and the greatest positive number gives an exposure E_2, the emulsion is ideally matched to the output.

exposures the only density involved is the slight absorption of the clear photographic base. At a critical exposure E_1, the curve begins rising steeply and with reasonable linearity until an exposure E_2 is reached. At this point, the curve flattens out and little further density results from longer or more intense exposures.

High-contrast films differ mainly in the range between E_1 and E_2. The maximum density obtained does not vary greatly and is adequate for all practical purposes. Consequently, the slope of the curve can be anything between 2 and 6, indicating the degree of contrast in the film. This slope is called the "gamma" of the material. It is to some extent dependent on the processing conditions used, but in the case of high-contrast materials the control that can be exercised by variations in processing is limited. This is notably different from low-contrast materials whose gamma can be varied over a wide range, but seldom exceeds 1.5.

To use high-contrast film one must first determine the range of intensities from I_1 to I_2 and choose a film with the same ratio of E_1 to E_2. The exposure time must next be varied until $I_1 \cdot t = E_1 : I_2 \cdot t = E_2$ when the film will "cut" levels below I_1 and record linearly up to I_2.

The films we use currently in Great Britain are not widely available in the United States; readers are advised to consult their manufacturer's literature to determine which films are readily available.

The photographic control of output with noncoherent processes has been used by Stephens and Rogers (1974) and Alqazzaz and Rogers (1975).

REFERENCES

Alqazzaz, L. and G. L. Rogers (1975). *J. Opt. Soc. Amer.* **65**, 695.

Stephens, N. W. F. and G. L. Rogers (1974). *Phys. Educ. (GB)* **9**, 331–334.

7

Spatial Modulation

The procedures described in the last chapter are rather like the old method of signaling along a telegraph wire using a key and direct current. In our case the telegraph key is leaky and there is a direct current flowing along the wire all the time. The key merely alters the level of the direct current and we have to strain at the receiving end to detect the changes.

Great progress was made in electrical communications when an alternating carrier was introduced, the amplitude of which was modulated with a key or with a microphone current. Not only did this allow a number of signals to be passed simultaneously along a given channel, but by tuning the receiver we could increase its sensitivity and reject irrelevant information such as the mean level of the direct current.

In optics a similar device is available to us. In this case, however, there are two ways to use it. We can adapt the time-to-space analogy entirely and present our signal as the modulation of a spatial carrier, that is, a grating. This and related methods using spatial coding form the subject of this chapter. Alternatively, we can subject our signal to a temporal variation of intensity that does not interact with the mean DC level. This procedure is ideal if electronic detection and processing is to be done. Another advantage is that it does not occupy part of the spatial pathway and is, therefore, more widely applicable. This forms the subject of the next chapter, which is the core of the book.

7.1. THE CONCEPT OF A "DILUTE" OBJECT

In optical methods, but particularly those involving spatial modulation, there is a great advantage in having a "dilute" object. Double-spaced typescript is a simple example. The system is normally digitized; that is, it consists of black and white only. Either 90% or more of the object area is black and 10% or less is white, or vice versa. One can have a largely black area with a number of luminous sources of different intensities that only occupy a minute fraction of the field. The night sky is an example of this.

The great advantage of the "dilute" object is that the significant information occupies only a small fraction of the field. Each significant point may therefore be replaced by a moderately extended spatial code without the danger of appreciable overlap with its neighbours. Correlation of the pattern so obtained with the chosen code will enable recovery to be effected without the DC bias term in the system contributing to the output. The coding is normally a noncoherent operation but in many cases the correlation is done coherently, giving rise to a so-called "hybrid" system combining coherent and noncoherent stages.

An electrical example of a dilute object is the output of a traditional radar station. This consists of a number of short pulses separated by long intervals of silence. After reflection, of course, the signal is more fully occupied, and its capacity for discrimination is directly related to the interval between pulses divided by the pulse width. But again the system is capable of development. The short pulse with the long interval calls for very high peak power in the transmitter, and this involves technical difficulties. A great deal of time and energy has, therefore, been given to the development of "chirp" radar, in which every pulse is temporally coded in a highly significant pattern (Klauder et al. 1960). In this way, the transmitter can be kept running for a much longer fraction of the repeat interval, yet highly significant timing can be derived by correlating the returning signal with a copy of the transmitter pulse code. In fact, some of the earlier examples of spatial modulation or coding were derived specifically to imitate "chirp" radar (Barrett 1972b).

7.2. SPATIAL CODING

There are a number of spatial codes available but not all of them are equally effective. We can explore this by using the notation of convolutions and correlations.

Suppose $g(x, y)$ represents the input signal and $h(x, y)$ represents the code. In most cases of practical importance $g(x, y)$ is dilute and $h(x, y)$ has only a limited lateral extent. The production of the coded signal is equivalent to the convolution of $g(x, y)$ with $h(x, y)$

$$g(x, y) \circledast h(x, y)$$

The standard process of decoding is to correlate this signal with $h(x, y)$ and, if the code is centrosymmetrical, this is equivalent to a convolution. The result of this process is

$$|g(x, y) \circledast h(x, y)| \circledast h(x, y) = g(x, y) \circledast |h(x, y) \circledast h(x, y)|$$

Therefore the recovered signal resembles the original signal if and only if

$$h(x, y) \circledast h(x, y) \to \delta(x, y)$$

a two-dimensional delta function.

In practice, the only code that obeys this precisely is the delta function itself, but this does not greatly help. Therefore, a value of $h(x, y)$ is selected that peaks very strongly at the origin and has a relatively weak "shoulder" near the central peak. Everything turns on the ratio of the energy in this central peak to the energy in the shoulder and on the degree of dilution of the object. If the fraction of the object occupied with significant information is small compared with the ratio of the peak energy to the shoulder energy in $h(x, y) \circledast h(x, y)$ the chances of useful recovery are high. Otherwise the chances progressively deteriorate.

A popular code is a zone plate, with about a quarter of the total energy in the central peak. Random dots have also been used, although if more than four dots are involved this code is less efficient. Lingren et al. (1974) have estimated that a dilute object occupying 5% of the available space has a good chance of recovery with a zone plate code. The case of a random dot code has been studied by Alqazzaz and Rogers (1975).

7.3. MODULATION ON A LINEAR CARRIER

A very early experiment in noncoherent recording on a linear carrier (grating) was conducted by Stroke (Stroke and Restrick 1965). The basic idea is to set a noncoherent self-luminous or diffusely scattering or reflecting object in front of an interferometer. Any individual point on the object produces a wavefront that is coherent as between different points on the spherical cap and can, therefore, give rise to a set of fringes in the interferometer. The contrast and extent of the fringes depends on the wavelength range of the source, and to get satisfactory results this wavelength range must be very small. Therefore, Stroke used a laser source with a moving diffuser which would destroy any lateral coherence in the beam while retaining its chromatic or longitudinal coherence.

Some other individual points will also give rise to interference fringes, but in general these will have a different spacing and orientation. If the composite set of fringes is photographed, the added *intensities* of the fringes give a Fourier hologram (Stroke and Falconer 1964) and the object can be recovered by Fourier transformation in a Fraunhofer diffraction apparatus. This is then a "hybrid" method.

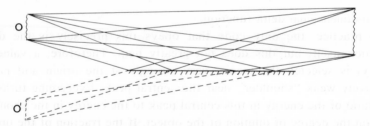

Figure 7.1 Use of a Lloyds single mirror to produce a spatial carrier wave, modulated by the Fourier transform of the one-dimensional object *O*. The light should be laterally noncoherent, but have a narrow wavelength range. The system was used by McIlraith to determine the partial coherence pattern of the object.

The simplest interferometer is a Lloyds single mirror, such as that used by McIlraith (1955) in studies on partial coherence (Figure 7.1). This will only work with a one-dimensional object set transverse to the mirror. To code and image a two-dimensional object on a photographic plate, a more complex interferometer is required which generates two images of each object point symmetrically disposed around a center of inversion. Stroke used a beam splitting grating and a system of mirrors.

Any beam inverting interferometer could, however, be used, including a Michelson interferometer with one mirror and one corner cube reflector or, any of the various wavefolding interferometers described by Mertz (1965).

The problem of chromatic coherence in spatially noncoherent interferometry has been tackled by Cozens (1976). He uses a type of Michelson interferometer to produce fringes from a one-dimensional object. The scale of the fringes depends not only on the position of an individual object point, but also on its wavelength. By arranging a pair of unequal diffraction gratings at an angle between the object and the interferometer, each individual object point is drawn out in a spectrum. In this way, the change of position with wavelength compensates for the wavelength, and the system can produce a large number of fringes in white light. The system is simply related to the production of achromatic fringes from the Lloyd single mirror by using an input spectrum rather than a line source.

7.4. INTERFEROMETRIC IMAGING

A development of the interferometer method has been proposed by Goodman (1970). The main difficulty with the method developed by Stroke is the weak contrast of the fringes produced, although the method of coherent reconstruction makes the best of such fringes as are present.

Goodman realized that if the object was accompanied by a small or point source of high intensity to one side, the point source would produce a basic fringe system of high contrast. It will be remembered that this technique assumes zero lateral coherence between the points in object space but considerable chromatic or wavelength coherence in the source. The addition of the object to the point source modulates the amplitude and phase of the basic fringe system in a manner analogous to the Leith and Upatnieks (1962) off-axis holography, which modulates the amplitude and phase of the biprism fringes that would arise if the reference beam were to cross an absolutely empty signal beam. The system has the additional attraction that, subject to not very restricting conditions, the method is insensitive to phase disturbances (e.g., atmospheric turbulence in the general region between the source and the interferometer). This is because there is no coherence between points on the object, so that shifts in the phase due to turbulence will not affect the recording of the intensity of the waves (Goodman 1970). This noncoherent method eliminates the effect of turbulence in much the same way as did the earlier coherent holographic methods developed by the same school (Goodman et al. 1966; Gaskill 1968, 1969; Goodman et al. 1969).

Rhodes in his thesis (1972) and in a paper with Goodman (1973) described a development of an idea that lies in the middle ground between coherent and noncoherent processing. Once again it is designed to eliminate the effects of atmospheric turbulence on a telescope by taking a number of short exposures of the object using different combinations of holes in a mask in front of the objective. Relative phases can be calculated by solving simultaneous equations, subject to an overall uncertainty in lateral position, and the "image" is put together on a computer from a reasonable sample of spatial frequencies. This can be described in terms of partial coherence (see Appendix V).

7.5. ZONE PLATE CODING

Pioneering work on spatial modulation and coding was done by Mertz and Young (1961) (Figure 7.2). The basic idea was to contribute to X-ray stellar photography. A map of the X-ray stars can in principle be obtained by a pinhole camera, but such a device is insensitive. To overcome this difficulty, Mertz made use of the fact that the X-ray star map is very dilute. Each star may thus be represented by a sizable code pattern without serious overlap. We have already seen that a zone plate is quite a good code. Thus using a zone plate mask in X-ray opaque foil in place of the pinhole of the camera we get a set of shadow zone plates. Since the X-ray wavelengths are very small the effect is purely geometrical because the zone plate focal length is several orders of magnitude longer than the camera. The density of the zone plate images are proportional to the intensities of the X-ray stars, and their centers map the star field. It is sometimes described as a noncoherent hologram, using an analogy due to Rogers (1950).

In order to recover the original signal we must correlate the output with the original code. It has recently been shown that this can be done

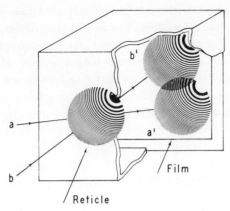

Figure 7.2   Diagram of the zone plate shadowing camera (after Mertz and Young).

in a noncoherent correlator (Silva and Rogers 1975) (see Section 4.4), though the contrast is very poor. It was noted by Rogers 20 years ago (Rogers 1956b) that the process of Gabor in line holography is equivalent to

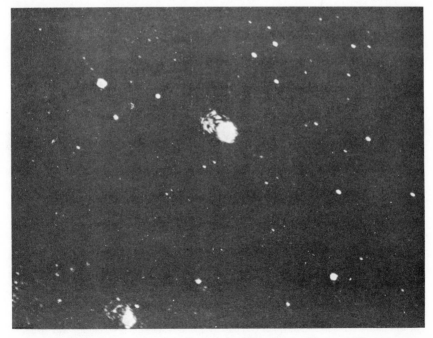

Figure 7.3   Plate showing the recovery of a star field with the Mertz and Young camera.

correlating the hologram with a complex-phase zone plate.† Hence in order to reconstruct the field, Mertz and Young (1961) used the Gabor "in line" technique. To facilitate this, the output pattern was photographically reduced to bring its diffractive focal length within the range of the laboratory. The focal length is proportional to L^2 where L represents the scale of the photograph. This effect was further helped by the change of wavelength from X-rays to light. It will be seen that this is a very early example of a hybrid system as well as a spatial code (Figure 7.3).

7.6. THE OFF-AXIS ZONE PLATE CODE

The process of "reconstructing" from a zone plate code creates the same "twin image" difficulty as found with in line Gabor holography (Bragg and Rogers 1951; Rogers 1956a). A zone plate has both positive and negative focal lengths so that energy is spread outward as well as being focused. Thus every point has a flare spot around it. The problem is not solved by the use of photographic clipping, because the weaker star images are lost in the clipping process.

To avoid the twin image a number of authors (Young 1963; Rogers et al. 1973; Barrett et al. 1972b) have used an off-axis zone plate analogous to the off-axis holography of Leith and Upatnieks (1972). This device has the effect of throwing the beam a known distance to one side as well as focusing it. The unwanted negative power in the zone plate is now associated with a deviation in the opposite direction, so that the unwanted blur halo clears the wanted reconstruction.

This particular technique works very well with an assembly of point sources, since each point source is equivalent to a wide range of spatial frequencies, and these frequencies interact with the zone plate to give a sharp shadow. Otherwise, the off-axis zone plate acts rather like a spatial frequency filter (Figure 4.3) and only parts of the shadows are sharp (Leifer et al. 1969), and then only if the appropriate frequencies are present in the object. An off-axis zone plate has a limited range of frequencies; in particular it has a low-frequency cutoff. If the object has no frequencies in the zone plate pass band it has to be modulated with a grating to give the correct frequencies before it is recorded (Barrett et al.

†In the particular application then discussed, a one-dimensional hologram was used, so that the correlation is with a one-dimensional section of a zone plate.

1972b). This is a further complication. The modulation not only reduces the intensity of the recording, but it involves holding a one- or two-dimensional grating over the object or between the object and the camera. However, the results obtained are most worthwhile with continuous tone objects.

7.7. CODING INTERFEROMETERS FOR ZONE PLATE CODES

Another way to superimpose a zone plate code on an input function is to use a special coding interferometer. Again a noncoherent object is used, preferably a dilute one that is mainly dark. Any individual object point produces a spherical wavefront, which is divided at a beam splitter. The wavefronts then pass through the system, and their curvatures are altered by a lens or lenses. On recombination, the system yields two mutually coherent wavefronts (for each object point) with different curvatures. These interfere to produce a zone plate pattern. The photographic plate sums these zone plate patterns in intensity, because the various object points producing them are mutually noncoherent.

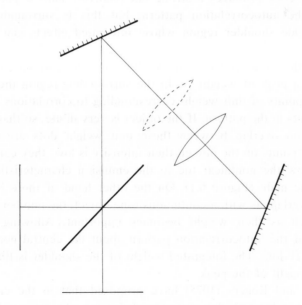

Figure 7.4 Triangular interferometer for spatial coding.

One of the neatest methods of zone plate coding employs a triangular modification of a Michelson interferometer (Peters 1966; Cochran 1966) (Figure 7.4). The beam is split into two halves which travel around the interferometer in opposite directions before being recombined at the beam splitter. By placing a lens asymmetrically in the system, two different curvatures are impressed on the two beams. It is convenient to place the output plane between the two images of the input produced by the system to give equal blur circles on the plate. Zone plate fringes are then formed within the blur circles. The lateral extent of the zone plate coding can therefore be controlled by adjusting the position of the lens. It should ideally be arranged to give relatively little overlap between adjacent points of the dilute object.

7.8. RANDOM DOT CODES

Another possible type of code is a random (or irregular) dot code. The basic idea is that the more unlikely the code the greater the correlation with the "key" when the correlator is brought into play at the decoding stage. Once again the question of dilution is crucial. This is because a random dot code produces a strong but relatively narrow peak at the origin of the autocorrelation pattern, but this is surrounded by a relatively wide shoulder region whose integrated effects can be considerable.

Thus if the code consists of N dots, its autocorrelation pattern consists of a peak of weight N. In the surrounding region there are a number of points of unit weight corresponding to correlations between distinct points in the pattern. If the object is very dilute, so that there is practically no overlap between these unit weight dots arising from neighboring points on the object, their intensity is low; they can usually be lost below the nonlinear toe to the emulsion characteristic of the photographic plate (Figure 6.1). On the other hand, if there is a considerable overlap, as with a continuous tone object, the number of these dots as well as their weight becomes important. Allowing for the symmetry of the autocorrelation pattern about the central peak, there are $N(N-1)$ dots. The integrated weight of the shoulder is thus $N-1$ times the weight of the peak.

Alqazzaz and Rogers (1975) have proposed that in the case of a continuous tone object, the central peak is an inadequate guide to the degree of recovery likely to occur. They have suggested drawing a circle, which they call the signal-to-noise ratio circle or SNR circle, that encloses half of the $N(N-1)$ dots on the shoulder. If we regard the data within this circle as a rather diffuse "point," then every point in the original input plane is replaced by a SNR circle in the output plane, plus a diffuse background of roughly the same weight. This gives a diffused output signal of the same magnitude as the background noise.

It is readily shown, again for a continuous tone object, that the size of the SNR circle is of roughly the same order of magnitude as the spread in the code itself. A point near the center of the random dot code projecting light through each hole of the second copy (Figure 4.2) will give a version of the code that will be substantially in the SNR circle. Dots to one side will give a version overlapping the SNR circle to some extent, so that some contribute to the SNR circle and some do not. Extreme dots will tend to contribute more to the shoulder. We see, therefore, that the SNR circle may be a little smaller than the original code, but that the recovery due to the correlation between output and code is not very great. This has relevance to certain procedures in X-ray and γ-ray imaging as well as to the question of deblurring.

7.9. EFFECT OF RECORDING NONLINEARITIES ON DECODING CODED PICTURES

The problem of the shoulder is much aggravated by the nonlinearity of the recording medium, especially where this is a photographic plate used with an input object containing a large number of resolvable points (say $>10^3$) or points to be recorded over a wide range of relative intensity.

The question is best illustrated by considering the zone plate shadow camera of Mertz and Young (1961). Let us suppose the image is built up by the successive exposure of the plate to the resolvable image points taken in sequence. The first point records the shadow of the zone plate in a position conjugate with the input point. Assume the exposure gives an image of adequate contrast, even if not very dense. The next image point superimposes another shadow zone plate and, for fairly small exposures, not around the toe of the characteristic curve, the effects are reasonably additive. This will hold as long as one is working on the middle range of the characteristic and the various points do not vary in intensity over more than say 10:1 range.

As the number of input points approaches the exposure range of the plate, which might be 500:1, we find ourselves on a portion of the characteristic curve that is flattening out. Additional points cannot now be expected to produce a proportional effect on the plate. The records they produce will introduce less change than those of the earlier points. The record is, therefore, degraded and unfortunately these extra points will tend to lessen the effect of the points already recorded. By the time we get to 5000 points, additional signals will have very little effect on an already overloaded plate, and 2 or 3 orders of magnitude later solarization will occur and additional points will actually *reduce* the signal. If we seek to record points with a widely differing range of intensity, say 100:1, these problems set in even earlier.

If we attempt to alleviate this difficulty at the high-exposure end by reducing the overall exposure of the picture, we get into trouble at the low-exposure end and lose information near the toe of the characteristic. In particular, relatively isolated or relatively weak points will fail to record.

In the case of X-ray and γ-ray records, the characteristic curves are different but still not linear. In this case, an additional source of trouble is photon noise. Even with an ideal recording medium, two signals will only add linearity if they are sufficiently free from photon noise (Dicke 1968; Lingren et al. 1974; Barrett and Horrigan 1973).

7.10. THREE-DIMENSIONAL EFFECTS

In X-ray astronomy, the stars are so far away that each zone plate shadow is of exactly the same size as the original. In reconstruction they will, therefore, all come to focus in the same plane.

In laboratory experiments, where the distance of the sources may be comparable to the length of the camera, each zone plate shadow is a magnified copy of the coding zone plate, and the degree of magnification depends on the camera extension and on the distance of the source from the camera. On reconstruction, the various zone plate shadows will focus at different distances from the plate and a three-dimensional representation of the original object will be formed. This will not be true to scale.

Suppose that P (Figure 7.5) is a source point, Z is the coding zone plate, and F is the recording film. P might be a localized concentration

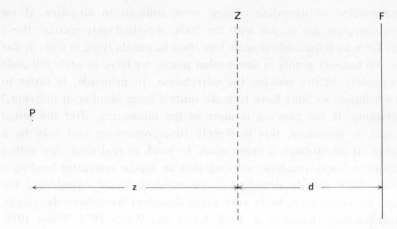

Figure 7.5 Three-dimensional effects in spatial coding. P = point element in source, Z = zone plate or other input code, F = plane of film or plate.

of γ-ray isotrope in a three-dimensional body cavity and Z might be cast in lead to give good shadowing properties (Barrett, 1972a; Rogers et al. 1972, 1973). If we take the distance from P to Z as the intrinsically variable distance z, and the distance from Z to F as the constant distance d, then the scale of the shadow is

$$\frac{d + z}{z}$$

times the original zone plate. This is a function of z. On reconstruction we get a constant scaling factor, depending on the photographic reduction between the recording film and the plate used for holographic reconstruction, and the "focal lengths" in the reconstruction apparatus thus vary as

$$\left(\frac{d + z}{z}\right)^2$$

The combination of the squared term with the fraction ensures that the reconstruction cannot be scale true in all three dimensions, except over a limited range if z is large compared with d.

The random dot code is also capable of three-dimensional effects. If a random dot (or hole) coder is placed in the plane Z of Figure 7.5 instead of the zone plate, then an enlarged shadow of the code is obtained on the film with a magnification $(d + z)/z$. This is also a function of z and is, therefore, sensitive to three-dimensional effects.

The process of decoding is now more difficult to visualize. If we simply correlate the output with the code, we shall only recover those points for which the code is scale true, that is, points lying in a particular plane. To recover points in some other plane, we have to scale the code appropriately before making the correlation. In principle, in order to scan a volume, we may have to make quite a large number of individual correlations. If the process is done in the laboratory after the initial exposure is complete, this is merely time-consuming and may be a nuisance. If an attempt is being made to work in real time, say with a multisource X-ray machine working into an image converter feeding a decoder, then speedy decoding is essential to avoid overdosing the patient. Consequently, some very rapid decoders have been developed for this purpose (Klotz et al. 1974; Klotz and Weiss 1974; Weiss 1974, 1975).

The process of decoding a random dot coded signal can be achieved by the "reversibility of rays" technique, described by Alqazzaz and Rogers (1975). In their paper, the system was originally described for a code plate at one end and the object between the code plate and the film. Similar considerations also apply to the case with the code plate between the object and the film. Thus, in Figure 7.5 if we simply replace the film and code plates in the original taking positions and arrange a diffuse source to the right of the diagram, the system becomes a projective type cross correlator between signal and code (Figure 4.2). However, in this case the projective magnification varies from place to place so the point of convergence of the cross-correlation pattern also varies. In other words, the cross correlation only works if the diffusing screen is placed in the correct position. The principle of reversibility shows at once that in this case the three-dimensional representation is scale true in all three dimensions, though location in the z direction may be inexact.

It goes without saying that these techniques depends very heavily on the object being exceptionally dilute. Not only must it be dilute in any one plane, but the whole system of points, if projected onto a single plane in space, must also be dilute. This is because out-of-focus points in addition to the shoulders of in-focus points contribute to the general background. In order to be able to take advantage of photographic clipping (Chapter 6), it is essential that the background due to all sources shall be kept very low. A more detailed discussion is given by Alqazzaz and Rogers (1975).

Consequently all these methods tend to be rather unpromising when faced with an object such as a γ-ray source of radioactive isotope in a diffuse and more or less continuous object such as the thyroid (Barrett 1972a; Barrett et al. 1973). On the other hand, when applied to X-ray imaging with dilute objects, such as a foreign body in an otherwise mainly open field, the technique can be very effective (Klotz et al. 1974; Klotz and Weiss 1974; Weiss 1974, 1975).

There is no doubt that a major advance in X-ray imaging has been achieved by the EMI X-ray scanner (Mersereau and Oppenheim 1974; Bracewell and Wernecke 1975). Although it is noncoherent this system is not truly optical data processing, because the effect is secured with a very complex computer program carried out by a specifically designed computer.

7.11. APPLICATIONS

7.11.1. X-ray Astronomy

Both methods of coding have been used in X-ray astronomy, where the very high dilution of the object is a tremendous advantage. Mertz and Young (1961) applied the zone plate method and Young (1963) developed the off-axis zone plate. Off-axis zone plate methods are analogous to the off-axis holography of Leith and Upatnieks (1962), and it is of interest that Young published so soon after the holographic work was completed.

The use of an irregular pinhole code was described by Dicke (1968). This paper gives a very complete analysis of the problems of the undilute object, and it shows that it is difficult to record satisfactorily more than 100 distinct, equally intense point sources with 10^6 holes in the code plate. If the sources are of unequal intensity further limitations occur. For example, if there are only *two* sources, an intensity ratio of 100:1 is the limit of detection. One of the basic assumptions made is that the total number of photons counted is less than half the number of code holes. For further details readers are referred to the original paper.

7.11.2. Diagnostic X-Radiography

Until recently, most diagnostic X-ray photographs have been straight shadowgraphs cast by an X-ray tube with a small focus shining through the patient onto an X-ray film. Various techniques have been developed to improve the overall performance. At the X-ray tube end there is a trade-off between spot size and beam current, since the heat generated at the focus must not exceed the capacity of the anode to dissipate it. Special devices, such as rotating anodes, have been developed to improve heat dissipation by constantly renewing the heated surface. At the other end, fluorescent screens (called intensifying screens) are placed in contact with the X-ray film so that the recorded image consists partly of X-ray fog and partly of optical fog caused by the light generated by the screens. Films with X-ray emulsions on both sides have long been used.

The development of the above ideas of optical processing leads to improvements in X-ray diagnostic imaging. The basic problem is to increase the X-ray flux without losing resolving power. Because of the physical limitations of anode materials, an increase of flux can only be achieved by an increase of spot size. If this is not to result in a loss of resolving power, the spot must be coded. Both zone plate codes and random or quasirandom codes have been proposed. In the latter case we can achieve the same effect as a larger spot by irregularly spacing a number of X-ray tubes of standard spot size.

Barrett et al. (1972a) have constructed an X-ray tube with a composite anode consisting of an aluminium base carrying a thin gold film etched in the shape of an off-axis zone plate. The area of this target is very much greater (~ 10.2 mm diameter) than the spot size conventionally used in X-radiography, and the zone plate has an average frequency of 27 line pairs/inch. X-rays are emitted copiously from the gold-plated regions of the target but very sparingly from the aluminium gaps. It is clear that if the object is dilute and consists of a few small holes in an otherwise opaque sheet, each hole will produce on the X-ray film a pinhole image of the anode, and this picture can be "reconstructed" in coherent light. With continuous tone objects the result is more difficult to obtain, since the pinhole images of the X-ray target become blurred. The focusing structure is thus lost and the reconstruction does not occur (Leifer et al. 1969). Barrett recognized this and covered his object with a fine halftone screen, photoetched out of gold and carrying 100 lines/inch. The object is therefore broken up into an array of fine pinholes, and although some overlap occurs, not all the spatial frequencies are lost (see Leifer et al. 1969 and Figure 4.3) and reconstruction is again possible. In theory, the pinholes should be small compared with their separations, so that the pinhole images are very sharp. The object then acts as a modulator, varying the relative intensities of these images.

In practice, a very fine pinhole array would once again lose photographic speed, so that in practice it is found that the pinholes may usefully amount to half the area of the screen, as used by Barrett. The main factor now is to choose the screen and target frequencies and the projective magnification factors that will constitute a tuned spatial frequency filter (Figure 4.3). It should be noted that a projective magnification term once again arises, so that three-dimensional reconstructions can be used.

The other technique of random sources has been developed by Klotz and his co-workers in the Philips Research Laboratory in Hamburg. Instead of using a random array of sources, Klotz and Weiss (1974) use what they describe as a nonredundant array. This is defined as follows. Draw a vector diagram representing the vector distances between each pair of holes or X-ray tubes in turn (i.e., an autocorrelation pattern), then a nonredundant array will have no coincident vectors and only the origin will represent more than one pair of points.

The X-ray picture produced by the nonredundant array of tubes is a composite picture of the subject produced by overlapping a number of different viewpoints. The number of tubes used was 10. The interest centers in the method of decoding or reconstruction. Since the object is three-dimensional, we have to perform a whole series of correlations, using the basic code pattern at various scales. A very ingenious use of holography enables this to be done rapidly.

In the first apparatus (Klotz and Weiss 1974) a Fourier transform hologram was made of the code point distribution with an off-axis reference beam. The reconstruction apparatus used a converging beam focused on the Fourier hologram and the coded X-ray picture is placed in this converging beam. By moving the X-ray picture along the axis toward the point of convergence, the relative scales of the point code pattern and the X-ray picture can be altered continuously. The reconstruction is viewed with a telescope at an angle to the axis corresponding to the angle of the off-axis reference beam used in making the hologram.

Such a hologram tends to be rather small, so the resolving power is limited. In a later development, Klotz et al. (1974) generate a large hologram by setting up the code pattern as an array of transparent glass beads in an opaque matrix and adding a reference bead to one side. The beads are illuminated with a laser, and a point hologram is produced at a reasonable distance away.

In the reconstruction apparatus, a zoom lens is used to produce a reduced image of the X-ray picture and this is used as a composite source for illuminating the hologram. It is only necessary to ensure chromatic coherence; the source can be laterally noncoherent, which is an advantage. The point hologram then gives a straight image on axis and a correlation off axis at an angle determined by the reference beam.

Klotz and Weiss use mainly objects with lead markers or foreign bodies, and these essentially dilute objects reconstruct well. They have also shown some results using a dummy hand which are quite promising. They believe that these results can be improved by increasing the number of X-ray tubes beyond 10. In view of the analysis of the SNR circle this is not necessarily correct.

It is theoretically possible that the X-ray pictures of Klotz and Weiss could be decoded by the "reversibility of rays" technique of Alqazzaz and Rogers (1975) but the contrast would probably be too low.

To avoid the delay and inconvenience of photographing the X-ray pattern and producing a scaled down transparency, Weiss (1974, 1975) has described a system using a Titus tube to interface with the optical processor.

7.11.3.   γ-Ray Imaging

A modern development in nuclear medicine involves the use of a radioactive trace element, often combined with a specific biological material, to outline some particular organ or diseased part. The use of iodine compounds suitably labeled to give an outline of the thyroid is a typical use of this technique which has formed the basis of a number of studies.

The traditional methods of producing images tend to be slow and to lack either resolving power or field area. An early technique was to provide a γ-ray detector with a narrow angle convergent collimator and scan it by hand over the thyroid area. The counts of each image point are typically stored in a computer and an image is plotted on a graph plotter. It is very difficult to build up a picture with a useful number of resolved points.

Another technique is to build up a bundle of narrow absorbing tubes between the γ-ray source and the detector, so that each point on the source can only irradiate one point on the detector. The tubes have to be very narrow but have walls thick enough to absorb γ-rays passing skew through the system. In general the arrangement is not very sensitive.

The third alternative is a pinhole camera using a narrow aperture in a lead shield. A useful summary of these techniques is given in Rogers et al. (1973).

The use of optical image processing techniques in this case is very similar in principle to the X-ray diagnostic case, except here the wanted information is in the source plane, and the coding system is placed between the source and the detector. The same basic systems are available: zone plate, off-axis zone plate, and random apertures.

A further complication arises that is much more serious in γ-ray-imaging than in X-ray diagnostic photography. The problem is the shot noise that arises from the individual nature of the photons employed. The energy of an individual photon goes up directly with frequency, so that hard γ-rays involve relatively few photons for a given amount of radiant energy. Statistical fluctuations in the number of γ-rays arriving at the detector in a reasonable recording time produce shot noise, resulting in a grainy or speckly image. The presence of shot noise imposes distinct limits on the product of resolving power by field size. In unfavorable cases a maximum of 100 resolved points is the best that can be recorded (Dicke 1968).

Rogers et al. (1973) have calculated noise effects in detail. They assume a photographic record, so that grain noise is the physical manifestation of photon shot noise. They show, as is now well recognized (Haine and Mulvey 1952) that the problem is much enhanced as the number of resolved points in the object is increased. If this number is M, these authors calculate that for noncoherent holography the noise goes up as M^2, whereas for coherent holography it goes up as M. They give as an example the parameters of a reasonable set up allowing a maximum value of $M = 550$.

Barrett and Horrigan (1973) also give a detailed discussion of noise and arrive at a similar result. They consider the increase of photon count necessary to maintain a given signal to-noise ratio as the resolving power is increased at constant field size. They conclude that with a pinhole or zone plate alike the count must go up as δ^{-4} where δ is the resolution distance. The number M of resolved points in the field goes up as δ^{-2}, so the counts must go up as the square of this to keep the statistical fluctuations $\alpha n^{1/2}$ to a steady level.

Lingren et al. (1974) have provided a detailed analysis of noise problems in zone plate imaging and in pinhole imaging. They relate their result to the "dilution" of the object; that is, they discuss the maximum proportion of theoretically resolvable points that can actually be occupied by a source. They conclude that the zone plate methods are superior to pinhole methods if the proportion of occupied sites is less than 5%.

The standard object used to test various methods of γ-ray imaging is the Picker thyroid phantom (Barrett 1972a). This is a purely artificial device with an agreed shape and size loaded with radioactive sources in a known manner. In general one lobe of the model is more highly radioactive, and both "hot" and "cold" spots are introduced into one or both lobes. This device has the great advantage that it is standardized for all laboratories and to shorten experimental times it can be loaded to a radioactive level higher than would be tolerated by a human patient.

A number of reconstructed images of Picker phantoms have been published. Most of these use the off-axis zone plate. An early paper by Barrett (1972a) uses an on-axis plate and a Schlieren stop in the reconstructing apparatus. Later papers by Rogers et al. (1973) and by Barrett et al. (1973) give results from off-axis zone plates. In all cases, some detail is resolved, but in these papers a direct comparison with a pinhole camera is not given.

More recent papers by Akcasu et al. (1974) and Koral et al. (1975) produce reconstructions by the random hole method. This development is very interesting, as the electrical pulses from the γ-ray counter are stored in a computer memory and the result is obtained by calculation. One of the problems with a so-called irregular hole plate is noise due to cross-correlations that are not quite uniformly distributed in frequency space. These authors have, therefore, used a random hole mask, which is moved across a limiting aperture in a number of steps during the exposure. Individual counts are made at each resolvable point in the detector plane for each position of the mask, and the whole matrix of information is stored. This is equivalent to performing the experiment 121 times and superimposing the 121 outputs to smooth out the noise. The amount of cross correlation between information stored and the hole code is phenomenal and the authors state that the time taken on their small Data General NOVA 1240 computer to recover the picture was 8 hours. It is, however, possible to reduce the computing time significantly by the use of a large, high-speed computer, and in view of the usefulness of the method, such a computer will undoubtedly be used in the future. The authors also publish a pinhole photograph of the same Picker phantom and the comparison is very instructive.

REFERENCES

Akcasu, A. Z., R. S. May, G. F. Knoll, W. L. Rogers, K. F. Koral, and L. W. Jones (1974). *Proceedings of the International Optical Computing Conference*, Zurich, I.E.E.E. No. 74 CHO 862-3C, 49–53.

Alqazzaz, L. and G. L. Rogers (1975). *J. Opt. Soc. Amer.* **65**, 695–699.

Barrett, H. H. (1972a). *J. Nucl. Med.* **13**, 382–385.

Barrett, H. H. (1972b). *Proc. I.E.E.E.* **60**, 723.

Barrett, H. H., K. Garewal, and D. T. Wilson (1972a). *Radiology* **104**, 429–430.

Barrett, H. H., D. T. Wilson, and G. D. De Meester (1972b). *Opt. Commun.* **5**, 398–401.

Barrett, H. H. and F. A. Horrigan (1973). *Appl. Opt.* **12**, 2686–2702.

Barrett, H. H., D. T. Wilson, G. D. De Meester, and H. Scharfman (1973). *Opt. Eng.* **12**, 8–12.

Bracewell, R. N. and S. J. Wernecke (1975). *J. Opt. Soc. Amer.* **65**, 1342–1346.

Bragg, W. L. and G. L. Rogers (1951). *Nature (GB)* **167**, 190.

Cochran, G. (1966). *J. Opt. Soc. Amer.* **56**, 1513–1517.

Cozens, J. R. and G. Wloch (1976). *Opt. Commun.* **18**, 307.

Dicke, R. H. (1968). *Astrophys. J.* **153**, L101–L106.

Gaskill, J. D. (1968). *J. Opt. Soc. Amer.* **58**, 600–608.

Gaskill, J. D. (1969). *J. Opt. Soc. Amer.* **59**, 308–318.

Goodman, J. W. (1970). *J. Opt. Soc. Amer.* **60**, 506–509.

Goodman, J. W., W. H. Hentley, D. W. Jackson, and M. Lehmann (1966). *Appl. Phys. Lett.* **8**, 311.

Goodman, J. W., D. W. Jackson, M. Lehmann, and J. Knotts (1969). *Appl. Opt.* **8**, 1581–1586.

Haine, M. E. and T. Mulvey 1952. *J. Opt. Soc. Amer.* **42**, 763.

Klauder J. R., A. C. Price, S. Darlington, and W. J. Albertsheim (1960). *Bell Sys. Tech. J.* **39**, 745–820.

Klotz, E. and H. Weiss (1974). *Opt. Commun.* **11**, 368–372.

Klotz, E., R. Linde, and H. Weiss (1974). *Opt. Commun.* **12**, 183–187.

Koral, K. F., W. L. Rogers, and G. F. Knoll (1975). *J. Nucl. Med.* **16**, 402–423.

Leifer, I., G. L. Rogers, and N. W. F. Stephens (1969). *Opt. Acta* **16**, 535–553.

Leith, E. N., and J. Upatnieks (1962). *J. Opt. Soc. Amer.* **52**, 1123.

Lingren, A. G., D. K. Julia, and J. E. Spence (1974). *Proceedings of the International Optical Computing Conference*, Zurich, I.E.E.E. No. 74 CHO 862-3C, 54–59.

McIlraith, I., (1955). *Proc. Phys. Soc. B (GB)* **68**, 1148–1150.

Mersereau, R. M. and A. V. Oppenheim (1974). *Proc. I.E.E.E.* **62**, 1319–1338.

Mertz, L. (1965). *Transformations in Optics*, John Wiley & Sons, New York, pp. 103–113.

Mertz, L. and N. O. Young (1961). *Proceedings of the I.C.O. Conference on Optical Instrumentation*, London, 305.

Peters, P. J. (1966). *Appl. Phys. Lett.* **8**, 209–210.

Rhodes, W. T. (1972). Ph.D. Thesis, Stanford University, Stanford, Calif.

Rhodes, W. T. and J. W. Goodman (1973). *J. Opt. Soc. Amer.* **63**, 647–657.

Rogers, G. L. (1950). *Nature* (*GB*) **166**, 237.

Rogers, G. L. (1956a). *Proc. Roy. Soc. Edinb.* (A) **64**, 209–221.

Rogers, G. L. (1956b). *Nature* (*GB*) **177**, 613–614.

Rogers, W. L., K. S. Han, L. W. Jones, and W. H. Beierwaltes (1972). *J. Nucl. Med.* **13**, 612–615.

Rogers, W. L., L. W. Jones, and W. H. Beierwaltes (1973). *Opt. Eng.* **12**, 13–22.

Silva, R. and G. L. Rogers (1975). *J. Opt. Soc. Amer.* **65**, 1448–1450.

Stroke, G. W. and D. G. Falconer (1964). *Phys. Lett.* **13**, 306.

Stroke, G. W. and R. C. Restrick (1965). *Appl. Phys. Lett.* **7**, 229–230.

Weiss, H. (1974). *Proceedings of the International Optical Computing Conference*, Zurich, I.E.E.E. No. 74 CHO 862–3C, 41–44.

Weiss, H. (1975). *I.E.E.E. Transactions on Computers* **C24**, 391–394.

Wilson, D. T., G. D. De Meester, H. H. Barrett, and E. Barsack (1973). *Opt. Commun.* **8**, 384–386.

Young, N. O. (1963). *Sky Telesc.* **25**, 8–9.

8

Temporal Modulation

The idea of temporal modulation first came into prominence in the 1930s with the early developments of infrared spectrometry. At first, infrared detectors were generally electrical, being either a thermopile or a bolometer; various semiconductor cells came into use later. In addition, the detectors were subjected to two sources of heat, the signal coming from the spectrometer and radiant heat from other parts of the apparatus. It is useful to be able to distinguish the two sources.

The method principally used in temporal modulation was to chop the signal beam by interrupting it at constant frequency with a fanlike system of rotating vanes. In this way the desired signal is characterized by a definite chopping frequency. A limit was set to this frequency by the time constants of the detector, but a bolometer will respond adequately to 100 Hz.

It will be seen that the problem of infrared spectrometry is very similar to the problem of DC bias. In the infrared case the DC is present as a constant background radiated by the nonfunctional parts of the apparatus, rather than a bias deliberately introduced, but its effect on the output detector is the same. In order to eliminate it, it is necessary to modulate the wanted signal without introducing the corresponding modulation into the DC background. This requires, for instance, modulation at the source and not at the detector. Modulation at the detector might well increase the sensitivity of the system, but it would involve measuring the DC level as well as the wanted signal.

The result of chopping is that the detector gives rise to an electrical signal that contains both an ac and a dc component. The former will be predominantly at the chopping frequency and can be isolated either with a tuned filter or by passing it through an isolating condenser. In this way the dc electrical component corresponding to the DC thermal background can be disregarded.

More sophisticated developments soon followed in which two optical paths could be balanced by switching light from one path to the other and minimizing the ripple between the two. A microphotometer using this principle was developed just before the war.

8.1.   THE PRINCIPLE OF TEMPORAL MODULATION

In general terms, temporal modulation is a periodic change of intensity superimposed on a particular signal to allow it to be distinguished from other signals in a system. In sophisticated arrangements, several signals may be used simultaneously yet kept separate by modulating each with a characteristic frequency. It is preferable that the frequencies used do not lie in any simple ratio to one another. This device is chiefly of use where the detector is electronic, giving rise to an electrical output that can be subjected to the necessary processing to separate the signals.

It would in principle be possible to combine this temporal modulation of a source with visual inspection through a stroboscope, but the technique is clumsy and I am not aware of its having been used.

There are three situations in which temporal modulation of the simplest sort can be applied. Setting aside for the time being the use of two or more modulating frequencies, we can first use a simple chopper. This is really a device for "labeling" the signal so that it can be recognized in the presence of a DC background. The object is to lose the DC background by suppressing the dc term in the electrical signal.

It is perhaps worth remembering that in an environment where many devices are being run off alternating current mains, it is by no means uncommon for sources of radiation to be modulated at mains frequencies (60 or 50 Hz according to country of origin) or, more commonly, at their second harmonic (at 120 or 100 Hz). Such sources of radiation can cause a disturbance at least as prejudicial as a steady DC background, and they may operate by adding an optical term to the light falling onto the detector, or by pure electrical breakthrough in an imperfectly screened circuit. It is, therefore, highly desirable to choose chopping frequencies well away from these mains-generated frequencies to enable electrical filters to separate the wanted signal from such spurious effects. Schemes have been proposed for increasing the chopping frequencies above mains frequencies by optical multiplication (Rogers 1970).

In the second use of temporal modulation, two optical paths are compared by switching. The object of the exercise is generally to produce an error signal that can be used to alter a variable component in one path to restore a balance. Variations in the second path are thus "followed" by the balancing component, and an output can be obtained from the position of the balancing component. In this application any DC background is again ignored by making no contribution to the error signal. On the other hand, any extraneous disturbance that happens to be modulated at the switching frequency will have a serious effect on the balance point, and it is, therefore, very necessary to be sure the switching frequency is well away from any mains-generated frequency.

A subsidiary use of switching is to economize on the number of photodetectors and avoid any relative drift between two or more. In this case, various inputs are switched successively onto a single detector (commonly a photomultiplier or other relatively expensive piece of equipment), and the electrical outputs, which may vary considerably, are picked up for separate processing by sampling switchgear (Cook and Richardson 1959; Cook 1960).

The third use of temporal modulation of the simple kind is more subtle. It occurs when an AC optical signal is superimposed on a DC optical background or bias, and it is necessary not only to separate the two but to measure the ratio of the AC element to the DC element. Important here is the measurement of optical transfer functions (Chapter 10). In this case we have to measure the contrast or visibility of the output when an input of 100% visibility is applied. The contrast is commonly defined as the Michelson visibility $V = (I_{max} - I_{min})/(I_{max} + I_{min})$, so that we need to measure the variation in the output $(I_{max} - I_{min})$ and compare it with the average DC level, $\frac{1}{2}(I_{max} + I_{min})$. It is therefore necessary to design our system of temporal modulation to give ac and dc electrical signals that are true to the corresponding AC and DC signals. This is typically achieved by the method of sequential switching (Rogers 1975).

8.2. THE METHOD OF SEQUENTIAL SWITCHING

The method of sequential switching, sometimes called sequential chopping, involves switching the illumination from one path to another in sequence, and allowing the energy to fall on a detector. There may be two paths, as in certain self-balancing systems, but more commonly there are several. The essential requirements are (1) there are no dark periods or overlap in between the various paths and (2) the paths are so arranged that the DC term in the optical system does not yield an ac electrical output but does give rise to a steady dc electrical output of the correct size. It is, in practice, very difficult to fulfill the first requirement with a vane chopper or switch, so that in practice a polarization system is preferred that gives rise to a steady cross-fading in the system and avoids transients as a solid chopper edge crosses the field (Jerrard and Sellin 1962).

One of the principal advantages of sequential switching is that by using more than two pathways, the position, that is, the phase, of an optical spatial frequency can be determined. If an optical spatial frequency exists, one way of detecting it is to scan a narrow line of light across the structure and measure the ac signal produced when the transmitted light falls on a photodetector. This is basically the technique used in measuring the O.T.F. of a lens, though one uses a narrow slit in front of the photodetector and an extended image scans across the slit. In either case, we get the very useful result that the ac term in the electrical system represents the optical AC signal, while the dc term in the electrical output represents the optical DC level. In this way, the visibility, or ratio AC/DC, is readily obtained.

Another way of measuring the AC/DC ratio is to arrange that the various pathways trace out a locus on a surface. The simplest case is a linear path across a plate or an output surface. If we seek to detect a spatial frequency in the output, we typically shift each pathway $1/n$th of the spatial period for each step. Then after n steps the pathway is returned to the start. If this spatial frequency is present in the output, an ac electrical signal is produced at the switching cycle frequency.

As a particular example of how this can be done consider the system illustrated in Figure 8.1. This consists of a screen built of a large number of strips of polarizing filter; the polarization direction of each strip is advanced 60° relative to the strip on its left and 60° behind the strip on the right. We have, therefore, a system with three possible pathways, the arrays specified by the letters A, B, and C. If an output shadow, such as that arising from a spatial frequency filter (Figure 4.3) falls on this system of polarizers in the correct orientation, the regions A, B, and C will be differentially illuminated.

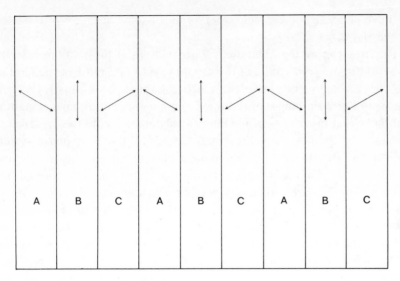

Figure 8.1 A composite polarizing filter used to achieve sequential switching. Regions A, B, C are polarized in different directions. A rotating polarizer "opens" each set of stripes sequentially and as a result a wave appears to pass across the surface of the composite filter.

To achieve sequential switching, we have only to combine this system with a rotating polarizer, which may be placed anywhere between the source and the detector. This causes the channels A, B, and C to open sequentially, with continuous cross fading in a cyclical manner. If A, B, and C are differentially illuminated by an output signal, this produces an ac electrical output from a photodetector arranged to integrate the transmission from the screen. On the other hand, a uniform (DC) optical illumination gives exactly the same signal whether pathway A, B, or C is open. This gives rise to a steady dc term in the electrical output. If the shadow is of low contrast, the electrical output is a mixture of ac and dc, and the visibility or contrast of the shadow can be measured by comparing the ac and dc components of the electrical signal.

It is now necessary to enquire why three channels A, B, and C are used. Would two not be sufficient? In practice, we assume the ideal shadow of 100% contrast has equal areas of black and white. If we have only two components in our composite polarization filter, the system will work if the black area falls on region A and the bright area on region B. But if the shadow is moved a quarter of a period sideways, the bright area will fall half on A and half on B and no ac signal results. Moreover, we have no means of knowing whether the shadow has moved to the left or the right.

The use of more than two areas corrects both of these failures. In the threefold system we can regard the pathways A, B, and C as generating the three components of an ac electrical three-phase supply system. Under uniform illumination the three components are in balance and no return current flows back along the neutral conductor. In the presence of a shadow of the basic system spatial frequency, the three-phase system goes out of balance and an output ac current appears in the neutral conductor. By making the photodetector integrate the light through the three regions we are effectively placing it in the neutral return circuit.

It is a further property of a three-phase system that the phase of the current in the neutral conductor indicates the nature of the imbalance between the three phases of the supply. It therefore indicates the spatial phase of the shadow, that is, its lateral displacement. This method can also be used as part of a moire pattern method of measurement or for the control of machine tools.

8.3. DESIGN CONSIDERATIONS

In summary we may say that design considerations require the following:

1. Temporal modulation involves a switching sequence giving a maximum interaction with the spatial frequency or other property of interest.

2. The modulation should give no electrical ac signal for DC optical terms.

3. The system may produce a dc electrical signal proportional to the DC optical signal for comparison with the ac/AC terms.

4. The frequency or frequencies chosen for operation should be well away from any mains-generated frequencies or other sources of interference.

5. With multifrequency systems, the frequencies chosen should not be simply related (to avoid harmonic interaction) and should be sufficiently distinct to be readily separated. It also follows that no frequency should be the sum or difference of two other frequencies in the group.

6. Great care is necessary to ensure that the luminous source is steady

and in particular free from any modulation on frequencies to which the system is sensitive.

8.4. MECHANICAL METHODS OF TEMPORAL MODULATION

8.4.1. Choppers

The simplest method of producing temporal modulation is by a rotating chopper. A selection of possible systems is shown in Figure 8.2. Generally speaking, one uses a balanced set of blades, or a circular disk with a balanced set of apertures. Simple blade choppers are useful where a source is modulated for coding purposes, as in I.R. spectroscopy. A system of apertures in a circular disk, may be used when it is desired to switch a beam from one route to another.

In all of these cases, it is highly desirable that the optical system does not form an image of the chopper edge on the final photodetector. If an image is formed the signal produced can be adversely affected by patches of high or low sensitivity on the photodetector surfaces. Ideally, the chopper should be placed in a plane orthogonal to the photodetector. When it is in this position, as the edge of the chopper advances across the beam the output intensity in the detector plane simply reduces in proportion, and its relative distribution over the surface is not affected. In the case of a disk that switches to two or more routes, this ar-

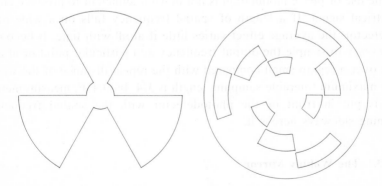

Figure 8.2 Two possible choppers. The three-bladed chopper is useful for the overall modulation of a source, as in infrared spectroscopy. The more complex chopper allows sequential chopping between three possible paths. In either case, the chopper should be in a plane "orthogonal" to the detector surface.

rangement is particularly desirable. If correctly adjusted the fall of intensity along one route is exactly balanced by the gain of intensity along the next route, so that the system produces no ac signal unless there is a lack of balance between the routes.

8.4.2. Gross Motion: Phase Modulation

In systems where the input consists of a spatial frequency, for example, the O.T.F. measurement discussed in Chapter 10, it is possible to modulate by giving the input pattern a gross motion sideways. This does not, of course, alter the numerical value of the spatial frequency, but it does alter its phase, which is a linear function of lateral displacement. In order to avoid running out of spatial frequency, the input stripes must be arranged on a continuous track, for example, a film loop. More commonly the stripes are arranged as radial markings along an annular track on a rotating disk. By making the annular track sufficiently narrow compared with its mean radius, the slight tapering of the black and white areas can be reduced to negligible proportions.

Considerable attention has been paid to constructing very accurate radial tracks for metrological purposes, and tracks up to 21,600 lines per revolution are available. The accuracy of marking can be well in excess of 1 second of arc. In practice, tracks with a moderate number of lines, say 1000/revolution, are most suitable for O.T.F. and allied measurements because diffraction effects are still quite small.

The use of phase modulation is not in itself sufficient to produce an ac electrical signal. If a length of spatial frequency falls on a wide photodetector, the average effect varies little if at all with time. It becomes necessary to sample the output frequency at a particular point or at any rate over a region small compared with the repeat distance of the wave. The maximum tolerable sampling length is $\lambda/4$. In O.T.F. measurement a slit is put in front of the photodetector with the spatial frequency running sideways across it.

8.4.3. The Wobbly Mirror

Another way of introducing lateral motion into the image of a system carrying spatial frequencies is to fold the optical path using a mirror spun about an axis that is not quite perpendicular to its own plane. This causes the image to describe a little circle, and, by allowing it to cross a slit or pinholes, an electrical signal can be generated in the photodetector. An equivalent method is to spin a thin prism in its own plane to give a periodic variation in image position. The method has been used in early experimental work but is clumsy in comparison with more recent optical methods. (Leifer et al. 1969).

8.4.4. Interferometers as Modulators

We have seen in the last chapter that a static interferometer can be used to produce spatial modulation. If one mirror of an interferometer is mounted on a transducer, such as a barium titanate piezoelectric cylinder, the interferometer can be used to produce temporal modulation. In this case, the interferometer is generally set with the mirrors parallel to give a uniform field free from spatial modulation.

Kozma and Massey (1969) have used such a modulator applied to one mirror of a Linnik interferometer to provide temporal modulation for holographic and data processing systems. As a result of such modulation a sinusoidal variation of phase is imposed onto the reference wave, and this is equivalent to using a series of Bessel functions to generate a whole set of sideband frequencies (as we shall see later). It is easier, however, to understand temporal modulation if we start by considering a single sideband system.

A. Macovski in his Ph.D. thesis (1968) has given a particularly useful survey of the use of temporal modulation. His primary interest is with holography, but he also discusses various schemes for deriving cross-correlations between a moderately large number of inputs, each labeled with a characteristic frequency. His work is thus developed in terms of coherent optics, but many of the basic principles and electronic techniques apply equally to noncoherent data processing. It is convenient, therefore, to develop the theory in coherent terms. The basic holographic technique using a plane reference wave is illustrated in Figure 8.3. It is based on the classical Mach Zehnder interferometer with the object taking the place of one of the corner mirrors. Temporal modulation is achieved by introducing a single sideband modulator into the arm carrying the reference beam. This is a polarization device, which will be described in detail in the section on polarization modulators, but its action is to increase or decrease the laser frequency by an amount corresponding to the rotational speed of a halfwave plate spun between

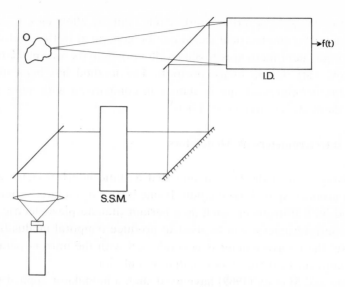

Figure 8.3 System used by Macovski for temporal modulation in holography. O = object, S.S.M. = single sideband modulator, I.D. = image dissector. The image detector does not integrate over a cycle but gives an output $f(t)$ depending on the instantaneous scan position.

two elements generating and reconverting circularly polarized light, respectively.

The hologram is formed on the cathode of an image-dissecting television camera. It consists of a conventional hologram with the fringes in constant and continuous motion due to the frequency offset of the reference wave, which is equivalent to a constant rate of change of the reference phase. It is, of course, essential *not* to use a storage television camera as this would integrate the fringe motion over several cycles and the effect of the temporal modulation would be lost. Any particular point in the hologram image will show temporal modulation as the fringes pass it. This modulation can be detected if the scan rate is either very slow or much faster than the modulation frequency.

To see what happens, we note that the intensity at (x, y) on the hologram is now time dependent where

$$I(x, y, t) = |Re^{i\omega t} + U|^2$$

where U is the object wave at the hologram plane which is a function of x and y but not t, and R is the amplitude of the reference wave at the hologram plane. R is a function of x and y but is not in itself a function of t. Its time dependence is represented by the multiplier $e^{i\omega t}$.

Multiplying out the right-hand side we get

$$I(x, y, t) = |R|^2 + |U|^2 + R^*Ue^{-i\omega t} + RU^*e^{+i\omega t}$$

we see, therefore, that the hologram terms are separated from the background terms by being temporally modulated through the multipliers $e^{\pm i\omega t}$. These have the same frequency but opposite rotational signs. Since R and U are both complex, we cannot separate them wholly on a single hologram, but various options are open to us.

1. We can couple the image dissector (scanning very slowly relative to ω) to a photorecorder through a band pass filter centered on ω and wide enough to pass all the video frequencies contained in U. This will generate a grating, corresponding to the modulation frequency ω, with amplitude and phase modulations corresponding to U. In other words, it generates a Fourier hologram, which gives two reconstructions in a coherent beam on either side of the axis and well separated. The technique makes great demands on the performance of both photorecorder and photographic plate, and is not really practical.

2. We may much reduce the demands made on both photorecorder and photographic material by lowering the carrier frequency ω to an intermediate frequency $(\omega_1 - \omega_2) < \omega$ using a heterodyning technique. The modulated video signal from the image converter is mixed with a local oscillator at ω_2. If we now call the original modulation frequency ω_1, we get new signals at $\omega_1 - \omega_2$ and $\omega_1 + \omega_2$. By a suitable choice of ω_1 and ω_2 we can separate the signal at $(\omega_1 - \omega_2)$ by a band pass filter centered on $(\omega_1 - \omega_2)$, subject to the requirement that $|\omega_1 - \omega_2| >$ bandwidth of the video signal from U. In this case, we get a Fourier hologram of carrier frequency $(\omega_1 - \omega_2)$ and this gives separation of the conjugate images, though they are now much nearer the axis.

3. We can employ a two-hologram method analogous to that used by Gabor and Goss (1966). They used a modified Mach Zehnder to produce two holographic records of an object. The amplitudes of the reference waves in the two holograms were carefully matched and their phases were shifted by 90°. By recombining waves from the two holograms in the same interferometer a complete reconstruction can be obtained, free from the conjugate image. The same apparatus or a device very similar to it, can be used to reconstruct from two holograms obtained from

the temporal modulation system. In this case, the video signal from the image-dissecting camera is divided into two. One signal is mixed in a homodyne detector with a reference signal $\cos \omega t$ and fed to one photorecorder. The second signal is mixed in another homodyne detector with a reference signal $\sin \omega t$ and fed to a second photorecorder. The two records contain the real and imaginary parts of U, respectively. As we now have no carrier frequency, the recording system and accompanying film only require the bandwidth or resolving power corresponding to U. This system can be used to separate the real and imaginary parts; for example, in the Fourier transform of a signal produced by noncoherent techniques.

Having discussed what happens in the simplest case of single sideband modulation we can now consider the more complicated result when the phase modulation is itself of sinusoidal profile. This can be produced by the physical oscillation of a mirror or by inserting an electro-optic crystal into one beam and imposing a sinusoidal voltage upon it.

In this case, instead of having a reference beam $Re^{i\omega t}$ we get $Re^{im \cos \omega t}$ where m is the depth of the phase modulation.

$$I(x, y, t) = |Re^{im \cos \omega t} + U|^2 = R^2 + U^2 + R^*Ue^{-im \cos \omega t} + RU^*e^{im \cos \omega t}$$

We can cope with this if we use the series expansion

$$e^{im \cos \omega t} = \sum_{k=-\infty}^{\infty} i^k J_k(m)e^{ik\omega t}$$

from which we see that not only does the frequency ω appear but also all its harmonics (i.e., $k\omega$).

It will also be noticed that because the term i^k occurs in the expansion, even harmonics correspond to real terms and odd harmonics to imaginary terms. If, therefore, we use homodyne detectors to separate the real and imaginary points, we must drive the real homodyne by $\cos 2\omega t$ and the imaginary homodyne by $\cos \omega t$, otherwise the technique for combining the separated holograms will be the same.

It also follows that should one desire to shift the signal to an intermediate frequency $\omega_1 - \omega_2$, it is not sufficient to heterodyne with a frequency ω_2. To get an equivalent result one must use a more complicated heterodyne signal, namely

$$p(t) = \sin(\omega_1 + \omega_2) + \cos(2\omega_1 + \omega_2)$$

This combines the real and imaginary parts in the required intermediate frequency.

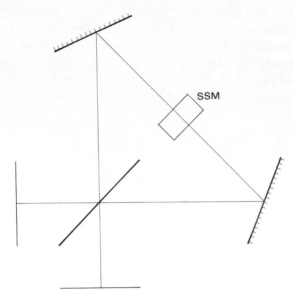

Figure 8.4 A triangular interferometer with a single sideband modulator to achieve temporal modulation. (Compare with Figure 7.4 for spatial modulation.)

Finally, it is interesting to note that the triangular interferometer used for spatial modulation (Figure 7.4) can be adapted to temporal modulation (Figure 8.4) by using a single sideband modulator instead of a lens. If a rotating halfwave plate is the active element of the single sideband modulator, it can be designed so that the wave traveling one way around the triangle has its mean (optical) frequency increased by ω, whereas the wave traveling in the reverse direction has its optical frequency lowered by ω. The two images of the object produced at the output, therefore, beat at a frequency 2ω and this can be picked up by the detection system.

8.4.5. Grating Modulators

We have already discussed the use of a grating, moving sideways, in our description on O.T.F. measurements. These modulators can also be used in a variety of other applications (West 1971). For example, they can be used to modulate light falling on a sheet of printed material to check it for registration. The method also lends itself to reading codes on packets of various items passing along a conveyor belt.

A grating has a dual purpose; it can be used as a beam splitter and as a modulator. Consequently, a grating can be used as an element in an interferometer. The straight through beam is unaffected in frequency whether the grating is moving or not. But the frequencies of beams on either side are modified, one being increased and the other decreased. In this way, many of the effects produced by the single sideband modulator can be reproduced.

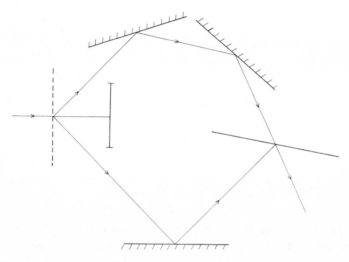

Figure 8.5 An interferometer that uses a moving grating as a beam splitter and a half-silvered mirror for beam recombination. This also gives temporal modulation.

Figure 8.5 shows a possible interferometer using a grating as a beam splitter and a half-silvered plate as a beam recombining device. It is necessary to have two reflections before the beam splitter in one arm and one in the other to avoid lateral invasion of the beam because the splitter laterally inverts one beam relative to the other. The grating will then work not only with a coherent beam but with a laterally noncoherent beam. The use of a grating does, however, restrict us to monochromatic illumination (longitudinal coherence) because the angle of deviation is a function of wavelength. Temporal modulation is superimposed on the system by moving the grating sideways. As with O.T.F. this is normally done by using a radial grating and illuminating only a small area on its edge.

The system has found particular application in holography. Mottier and his colleagues (Mottier 1974) have developed a system of frozen fringe holography wherein the frozen fringes can be made to move by moving a grating in the reconstruction setup. In this way, the frozen fringes are temporally modulated, and the phase relations between various points of the field can be determined by an electronic phase meter driven from two photodetectors. One photodetector is normally kept fixed at a point of the field arbitrarily designated as the zero of phase, while the other is allowed to scan the field very slowly until a phase map has been built up. In visual frozen fringe work it is normally possible to make a reasonable estimate to a tenth of a fringe, which is equivalent to 36°. The use of an electronic phase meter can allow phase measurements to better than 1° provided sufficient integration time is available. The use of electronic techniques thus greatly increases the accuracy of measurement over visual methods.

8.5. OPTICAL METHODS OF TEMPORAL MODULATION

8.5.1. Polarization Modulators

Problems of mechanical motion can be avoided by the use of electro-optic modulators where an electrical signal alters the state of polarization of a beam. Such devices can be operated at several mHz. Polarization modulators have the considerable advantage that because a moving edge is not involved, shadowing does not occur. For many purposes where very high-frequency operation is not required, mechanically driven polarizing disks can be employed to great effect.

An early example of polarizing disks was the Jerrard and Sellin chopper mentioned earlier (Jerrard and Sellin 1962). In its original form the rotating polarizing disk was used with a further fixed sheet of polarizing material to give a sinusoidally varying overall transmission. The system can be readily adapted to use with a double beam self-balancing system by replacing the second fixed polarization filter with a polarizing beam splitter.

In this case, the incident beam is divided between the two paths by the beam splitter, and the fraction of the energy going down each path depends on the direction of the rotating polarizer at the given instant relative to the two polarization directions of the beam splitter. The fraction will, therefore, vary between the two beams as the rotating polarizer revolves. Each output beam will exhibit a sinusoidal variation of intensity, but the beams will be in antiphase. If, after traversing the two paths, the beams are mixed on a single photodetector they will give a sinusoidal ac signal unless the two path transmissions are exactly balanced in which case no ac electrical signal will result. The phase of any ac signal arising from a lack of balance will depend on which path has the higher transmission, and hence when fed into a phase-sensitive detector it will give an error signal. This error signal can be made to operate a servo loop to restore the balance.

The output of a rotating polarizer can also be made to switch energy sequentially along a succession of possible channels or paths A, B, C, and so forth, as in Figure 8.1. This will be discussed further under the optical selsyn.

8.5.2.   The Jaumann Modulator

As mentioned above, it is desirable to arrange the modulation frequency to be well away from any mains-generated disturbance. In the case of a polarizing disk driven by an induction motor, it generally happens that the system will settle down at a speed slightly slower than the mains frequency. This is also, of course, the frequency of the thermally introduced ripple on an ac driven lamp. Since the frequencies are nearly but not quite the same, very unpleasant beating effects can occur. This procedure of driving a servo loop off a chopping frequency nearly the same as possible mains disturbance can be used as a diagnostic tool to detect a lack of electrical screening. It is, however, wiser to avoid such problems than to compensate for them later.

The basic technique for avoiding close clashes is to use a device developed by Jaumann (Jaumann 1891). Originally designed for velocity of light measurements the device consists basically of a polarizer followed by a rotating halfwave plate. (Figure 8.6a). A halfwave plate has the property that a plane polarized beam of light (preferably of a fairly narrow wavelength range) emerges from it as a plane polarized beam, but with its polarization direction "reflected" in the fast axis of the halfwave plate. A fixed polarizer followed by a halfwave plate rotating at an angular velocity ω gives rise to a plane beam with its direction of polarization rotating at an angular velocity 2ω.

Jaumann proposed to use this to measure the velocity of light as

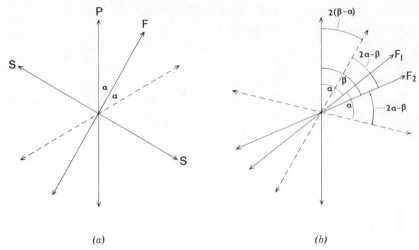

(a)   (b)

Figure 8.6   Jaumann modulator. (a) Effect of a fixed halfwave plate in "reflecting" the input polarizing direction P into the dotted position. F and S are the fast and slow axes of the halfwave plate. If the angle α is changed (e.g., by rotation at an angular speed ω), the dotted output plane of polarization rotates at an angle 2ω. (b) Use in measuring the velocity of light. F_1 gives the position of the fast axis as the light passes out through the halfwave plate. By the time the light returns from a distant mirror, the fast axis has moved to F_2. This means that the returning light emerges at an angle $2(\beta - \alpha)$ to the initial direction, whatever the phase of rotation (i.e., whatever the instantaneous value of α). All we require is that $\beta - \alpha$ is constant and this depends on the transit time of the light.

follows. Suppose the emergent beam is reflected by a mirror placed immediately after the rotating halfwave plate. Suppose at a particular instant of time the angle between the fixed polarizer and the fast axis is α. Then the angle between the fixed polarizer and the direction of polarization of the emergent beam is 2α. After reflection in the mirror the beam comes directly back through the halfwave plate. On entering the halfwave plate a second time, the beam is polarized at an angle α to the fast axis and emerges parallel to its original direction.

Suppose, however, the beam is reflected from a mirror 300 meters away. By the time it has gone out and back the halfwave plate has moved on to make an angle β with the fixed polarizer. The angle of the beam reentering the plate is now $2\alpha - \beta$ and on "reflection" in the fast axis the beam is displaced a distance $2(\beta - \alpha)$ from its original direction. This angle can be measured by a rotatable analyzer; the velocity of light can be measured in terms of the angle, the distance, and the angular speed of the rotating halfwave plate. The system has the advantage of being constantly open to the light, unlike systems using cogged wheels or rotating mirrors or polygons.

The rotating halfwave plate device can be used in a number of ways. For example, a whole set of them can be run in series to give a constant increase in angular speed. Figure 8.7a shows a series of halfwave plates arranged on two counterrotating shafts. A beam of light passing through the halfwave plates in series picks up an additional angular spread of 2ω at each pass. A modification (Figure 8.7b) shows the effect of fixing one of the rotating axes. In either case a useful increase of angular frequency can be obtained and beats between mains interference and the speed of an induction motor can be avoided (Rogers 1970).

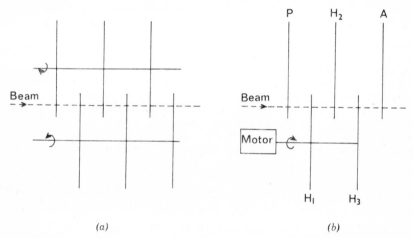

(a)   (b)

Figure 8.7 Multistage Jaumann modulator (a) with two counter-rotating shafts for the maximum effect, and (b) with one set of halfwave plates fixed for convenience.

A halfwave plate depends on having a plate of birefringent materials whose thickness and refractive indices satisfy the equation

$$\lambda/2 = t(\mu_e - \mu_0)$$

It follows that once the thickness t has been fixed, the operative wavelength λ is also fixed. In practice there is a certain range of acceptable wavelengths. If a single halfwave plate is involved, acceptable tolerances allow a useful range of wavelengths to be used. However, if one is using a whole series of halfwave plates the tolerances on each must be correspondingly tightened, and the system will work best with monochromatic light.

Much visual work can be done with a halfwave plate that is satisfactory over a wavelength range of 500–600 nm. Multistage systems require a correspondingly reduced range. Electronic systems also require special attention. In this case the sensitivity curve of the photodetector must be combined with the radiant efficiency curves of the light source to find the effective wavelength of the band in use. Both the polarizers and the halfwave plate must be chosen to fit this band. In many cases it is found that the system is working with high efficiency in a band from 700–900 nm (i.e., in the near infrared) and that the efficiency falls off outside this band. Infrared polarizers can be obtained to work in this region, and are essential for Faraday effect modulators (Stephens 1971). It is easier to buy halfwave plates in the visible, and it may be desirable to use a blocking filter to remove the infrared, so as to work in the red region from 600–700 nm.

A useful Jaumann modulator can be produced by spinning a halfwave plate in the hollow rotor of an air turbine (Rogers 1971). Alternatively the system can be made to operate over a wider wavelength range by spinning a polarizer in an air turbine, though in this case the angular velocity of spin is only ω and not 2ω.

8.5.3. Single Sideband Modulators

A useful single sideband modulator using polarization effects is described by Macovski (1968). To explain the action of the modulator, consider first Figure 8.8a, which shows an optical system sometimes called the circular polariscope. The element A is a linear polarizer passing light with a vertical component only. B is a quarterwave plate with its fast axis at 45° to the vertical. D is another quarterwave plate with its fast axis at 45° to the vertical on the other side. Thus B and D are "crossed"; the fast axis of one is parallel to the slow axis of the other. It is not essential that they cross, but it has the advantage of extending the wavelength range that can be used satisfactorily. The final element E is a linear polarizer. If E passes vertical vibrations, a maximum of light passes, but if E is set horizontal, no light passes.

If a birefringent specimen is placed in between B and D, with E horizontal (as drawn), light passes and the intensity of light passed is a

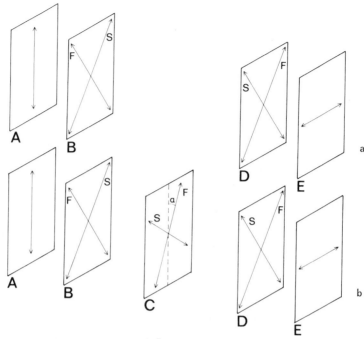

Figure 8.8 Construction of a single sideband modulator. (*a*) Circular polariscope. A = polarizer, B = quarter wave plate, D = second quarter wave plate, E = polarizer giving extinction. A birefringent specimen placed between B and D will allow light to pass, whose intensity is independent of the direction of the optic axis of the plate but whose phase is dependent on it. (*b*) The circular polarizer with a halfwave plate C inserted between B and D with its fast axis at an angle α to the vertical. The intensity of the light is now a maximum and the phase depends on the angle α. Steady rotation of C causes a phase shift equivalent to generating a single sideband from the input light frequency. The system is reversible, the opposite phase shift being produced in a beam traveling in the opposite direction.

function of the birefringence of the specimen. It is not, however, a function of the *orientation* of the specimen. In photoelastic analysis where one wishes to measure the stresses in a mechanical model, this property can be important. The mechanical model is made of a transparent material that becomes birefringent when stressed, and a circular polariscope will measure the absolute value of the stress (by measuring the birefringence produced) independent of its direction.

The system AB of polarizer and quarterwave plate generates circularly polarized light, while the system DE will only accept circularly polarized light. In the case illustrated, AB generates right-handed circular light, while DE accepts only left-handed. No light, therefore, passes. Since the vibrations between B and D have circular symmetry, the effect of a birefringent plate is independent of the orientation of the fast axis of the plate.

In Figure 8.8*b* we have introduced a halfwave plate C with its fast axis at an angle α to the vertical. The effect of a halfwave plate is to convert right-handed polarized light into left-handed polarized light, so that the system now transmits polarized light freely.

It is shown in Appendix IV that the *intensity* of the light passed is independent of the angle α, but a detailed wave analysis in terms of complex amplitude will show that the *phase* of the emergent wave is a function of the angle α. If now C is spun steadily the phase of the emergent wave shifts steadily and this is equivalent to a shift of the mean frequency. The shift is in one direction only, depending on the direction of spin.

It can also be shown that if C is spun so that it increases the frequency of a beam of light traveling in the direction ABCDE, it will decrease the frequency of a wave traveling along EDCBA. Thus if the single sideband modulator is placed in a triangular interferometer (Figure 8.4) it will produce temporal modulation between the two beams. A similar effect can be produced by inserting a linear polarizer in position C, although in this case the intensity of the emergent light is halved owing to absorption in the polarizer.

A quite independent method exists for producing a single sideband modulation. This requires the use of a linear electro-optic crystal, which introduces a phase shift into a suitably polarized beam, when subjected to an electric field. The effects tend to be small, so that quite high voltages are required. Nevertheless, by the use of the Pockels effect, or by the rather peculiar action of the Hexamine modulator, it is possible to produce phase shifts of half a cycle. Since the effects mentioned are linear and thus reversible, it is possible to produce either a retardation or an advance according to the direction in which the voltage is applied. The electro-optic crystal is connected to a ramp generator that swings the voltage steadily from $-V$ to $+V$ and then collapses rapidly to generate a continuous change of phase from $-\pi$ to $+\pi$ with a sudden reversion to $-\pi$. The sudden reversion from $+\pi$ to $-\pi$ is equivalent to zero change of phase, so that the phase of the wave is continuously advanced; that is, its frequency is increased (Figure 8.9).

It must be borne in mind that the ramp generator must work over the

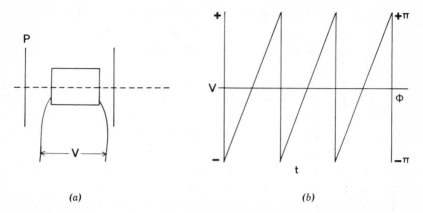

(a)   (b)

Figure 8.9   A continuous phase advance generated by a saw-toothed voltage drive on a Pockels cell (electro-optic crystal). (*a*) Optical and electrical arrangement of the cell. (*b*) Saw-toothed drive wave, which must switch the phase shift from $-\pi$ to $+\pi$.

range $\pm V$, where V is the voltage to produce a phase change of π—normally called the $\lambda/2$ voltage or halfwave voltage. This voltage may be several kV, so that a complex electronic arrangement is involved. If the capacity of the crystal between its electrodes is high, the power requirements become significant.

It is also a matter of rather fine adjustment to keep the peaks of the saw-toothed wave in the right place. Otherwise the jump is no longer from $-\pi$ to $-\pi$, and hence there is no longer a zero phase shift at the instant of flyback. This can considerably affect the emergent light, which now contains not only the shifted frequency but a collection of harmonics on the drive frequency. Consequently, some care is needed in controlling the electronics to give the best effect. The problem of matching the swing to the needed shift from $-\pi$ to $+\pi$ is complicated by the fact that the halfwave voltage is a function of temperature and there will, therefore, be a drift if the modulator heats up while running.

In view of the difficulty of matching the two ends of the saw-toothed wave, there is a good case for abandoning the single sideband principle and applying a sinusoidal voltage. This produces a phase shift represented by $e^{im\cos\omega t}$, which can be used for many practical purposes. This is equivalent to a set of Bessel functions, as discussed earlier under interferometer modulators. Although more complicated than single sideband modulation, the sine wave driven system produces satisfactory results. It has the further advantage that the depth of modulation m can be lower than for a saw-toothed drive. This means a lower voltage is needed and a special generator is not required. A step-up transformer from the ac mains is often sufficient, unless a number of different frequencies are to be used.

8.5.4. Electro-Optic Rotators

It was mentioned earlier that interesting and useful effects can be produced by using a beam of plane polarized light whose plane of polarization steadily rotates about the direction of propagation. Such a beam may be allowed to fall on a switching system that directs the main energy sequentially along a number of possible paths. The usefulness of these rotating systems can be greatly extended if the speed of rotation can be pushed up beyond mechanical limits into the 100 kHz–2 mHz region. The high speed of the electro-optic effect allows this to be done.

The simplest electro-optic rotator depends on the same sort of crystal modulator used in the single sideband system with the saw-toothed drive. It is only necessary to mount the modulator in the correct polarization train to get the required effect.

Figure 8.10 shows the system employed. A is a linear polarizer, with its polarization direction vertical, and B is the electro-optic modulator, arranged with its axes at 45° to the polarizer direction. It is impossible to say at this stage which axis will be fast and which slow, because this depends on the direction of the applied voltage. With zero voltage the

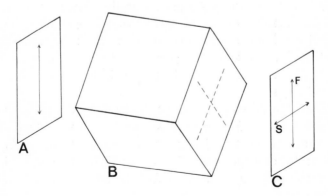

Figure 8.10 Combination of saw-toothed Pockels cell with a quarter wave plate to produce an electro-optical rotator. A = polarizer, B = Pockels cell with its induced fast and slow axes at 45° to A, C = quarter wave plate with its fast axis parallel to A.

axes disappear and the crystal is isotropic; that is, it has zero bire-fringence.

When a voltage is applied, the plane polarized wave is converted into an elliptically polarized beam. It is a peculiarity of this special arrangement (when the fast axis is at exactly 45° to the polarizer direction) that the axes of the emergent ellipse are always parallel to and perpendicular to the polarizer direction, that is, vertical and horizontal. If the applied voltage is low, the major axis of the ellipse will be parallel to the polarizer direction, that is, vertical, and the ellipse will be long and thin. As the applied voltage increases towards the quarterwave voltage, the ellipse fattens; it becomes a circle at the quarterwave point. Between the quarterwave voltage and the halfwave voltage the major axis of the ellipse is now nearer the horizontal, and at the halfwave point the emergent light is linearly polarized in a direction perpendicular to the polarizer A.

The effect of reversing the direction of the applied voltage is to reverse the direction of rotation of the polarized beam, that is, to change it from right-handed polarization to left-handed polarization.

What we require is a linearly polarized output at a variable angle to the vertical. To achieve this we use the fact that a quarterwave plate will convert an elliptically polarized beam into a linearly polarized beam if its axes are parallel to the axes of the ellipse. In general, the axes of the ellipse swing around as the voltage is applied to the crystal, but we have already seen that in the case of a 45° angle between the polarizer direction and the modulator crystal axes this no longer occurs. We can, therefore, insert a quarterwave plate C in the system with its fast axis vertical (i.e., parallel to A). In this case, the light emerging will be linearly polarized in the direction of the diagonal of the rectangle formed by the vertical and horizontal tangents to the ellipse. There are two such diagonals: one corresponds to right-handed ellipses and the other to left-handed ellipses.

All we have to do now is to drive the modulator with a saw-toothed wave from $-V$ to $+V$, where V is the halfwave voltage. This will steadily rotate the output polarization from horizontal to vertical ($V = 0$) and then into the other quadrant. The sudden flip from $+V$ to $-V$ leaves the output momentarily horizontal, so that the effect is of a continuously rotating vector.

A more complicated system has been developed by the Phillips Research Laboratories. This employs a train of three electro-optic modulators to convert circularly polarized light into linear polarized light with a rotating polarization direction. Its main advantage lies in the use of a lower drive voltage. The complexity of the system is considerable and it also has the disadvantage that very small nonuniformities arise in the speed of rotation (Peek et al. 1969).

8.5.5. The Optical Selsyn

It has already been pointed out that if a grid is made with successive strips A, B, C, A, B ... of polarizing material, with their vectors advancing 60° at each stage, it can be used to detect an optical spatial frequency corresponding to the distance A–A by introducing a rotating polarizer into the system. The integrated output is detected by a photocell. If a signal exists the output will have an amplitude corresponding to the contrast of the signal and a phase corresponding to the phase of the signal, measured from a zero defined by the rotator.

It is exceedingly inconvenient to have to construct a grid with a large number of strips of polarizing material, especially if the scale is small. An equivalent system can readily be produced by gathering all the "A" strips into one corner of the grid, and representing them by transparent lines on a dark ground. A suitably orientated polarizer is then placed over the region. The "B" strips are now isolated in another region and are represented by transparent strips as before, except that the phase of this grid has been shifted a third of a period sideways, relative to the "A" strips. The "C" strips are similarly collected together.

Figure 8.11 shows the effect. A master grid was constructed on a very large scale and photoreduced. The great advantage of this system is that different optical frequencies can be accommodated by making a series of photographic reproductions on appropriate scales. The necessary polarizers can be produced by cutting a sheet of polarizing material into sets of 30°, 60°, and 90° triangles and mounting them suitably over the different areas.

A circular photodetector can be located behind this composite grid and centered to give equal areas of the A, B, and C regions on its surface. The boundary between A and B is arranged at right angles to the boundary between C and the other two regions. In this way, it is possible to compensate for small variations in photodetector sensitivity over its surface by small displacements parallel to one or both boundaries.

Figure 8.11   Split grid used in the optical selsyn. The regions A, B, and C are phase shifted by a third of a period and suitable polarizers are inserted.

The fact that the boundaries are perpendicular means we can alter the percentage contribution of C to the system without altering the ratio of A : B, or vice versa. The system has been developed in the Aston character reader (Chapter 10).

REFERENCES

Cook, A. H. (1960). *Optics and Metrology*, Pergamon Press, Oxford, 259–268.

Cook, A. H. and H. M. Richardson (1959). *Proc. Phys. Soc. London* **73**, 661–670.

Gabor, D. and W. Goss (1966). *J. Opt. Soc. Amer.* **56**, 849–858.

Jerrard, H. G. and O. O. Sellin (1962). *Appl. Opt.* **1**, 243.

Kozma, A. and N. Massey (1969). *Appl. Opt.* **8**, 393–397.

Leifer, I., G. L. Rogers, and N. W. F. Stephens (1969). *Opt. Acta* **16**, 535–553.

Macovski, A., (1968) "Efficient holography using temporal modulation." Ph.D. Thesis, Stanford University. (University Microfilms, Ann Arbor, Michigan).

Mottier, F. M. (1974). *International Optical Computing Conference*, Zurich, I.E.E.E. No. 74 CHO 862-3C, 69–72.

Peek, T., H. de Lang, and G. Bouwhuis (1969). *Laser and Opto-Electronics Conference*, Southampton. S177.

Rogers, G. L. (1970). *Appl. Opt.* **9**, 2396.

Rogers, G. L. (1971). *Proceedings of the Electro-Optics International Conference*, Brighton, 365–368.

Rogers, G. L. (1975). *Opt. Laser Tech.* **7**, 153–162.

Stephens, N. W. F. (1971), Ph.D. Thesis. University of Aston, Birmingham, England.

West, P. (1971). *Metron*, **3**, 186–192.

9

Electronic Methods
for Processing the Signals
Derived from Optical Systems

One of the great advantages in converting optical information into electrical signals is the ease with which electronic means can be used to manipulate the information. In the simplest cases we require merely to suppress the dc term in the electrical output. In more complex cases AC and DC optical terms have to be treated separately or their ratio established. Further applications of electronic processing include thresholding, digitizing, and the application of logical processing, for example, in decision making in a character reader.

9.1. SUPPRESSION OF THE DC LEVEL

The DC level in a piece of optical apparatus, for example, an infrared spectrometer, can be suppressed by blocking the corresponding dc electrical signal with a blocking condenser. This can in principle, be placed anywhere in the amplifier circuit, although it is normally placed as early as possible to prevent the amplifier from saturating. In practice a number of points require attention.

In the first place care must be taken to ensure that the DC light level is not so high that the photodetector saturates. A few photodetectors have a very large linear range, such as the device described by Phelan (1973). This has been calibrated by the use of dc electrical heating to simulate the incident radiation, and has been found linear over six decades in incident power. Photodetectors of the semiconductor photovoltaic type are less linear but still very useful, besides being reasonably sensitive. More complex systems, such as television cameras that combine detection with scanning, have more limited range: a range of two decases would be typical. At the high sensitivity end, photomultipliers are linear over a relatively high range, provided the drive voltages are stabilized as is normally possible with modern voltage control of the supplies. In this case, the main limitation at the low energy end arises not so much from any lack of linearity as from the appearance of photon noise.

A photomultiplier can respond to a single photon, although it does not always do so because its quantum efficiency is less than perfect. At low intensities, photons do not arrive at an absolutely uniform rate, hence one has to employ time-averaging techniques to reduce the effects of these irregularities.

In these simple situations, one is looking for an ac ripple superimposed on quite a considerable dc level. Hence the cell must be linear and not saturate. For example, we find an optical selsyn working into a solar cell will work quite well in diffuse laboratory lighting, but if we allow strong daylight into the laboratory the cell saturates and the ac signal becomes difficult to isolate.

Although blocking condensers are by far the simplest and most widely used devices, a coupling transformer will also block dc. Problems, however, arise from the limited band pass and tendency to resonate found in most coupling transforms.

9.2. RETENTION OF dc TERM–AVERAGING PROCEDURES

When it is desired to measure the AC/DC ratio of an optical signal, it may be necessary to retain the dc component of the corresponding electrical signal, though there may be ways around this requirement. The simplest way of retaining the dc is to average out the effect of the ac ripple by a standard CR integrating circuit with a time constant very much higher than the period of the ac ripple. Once again a choke can be incorporated but it generally offers no advantage.

In systems that are required to respond rapidly to external changes, such as control systems and character readers, it is not possible to use an integrating circuit with an indefinitely long time constant. The time constant must, therefore, be designed to be comfortably less than the response time required of the system as a whole. This in turn imposes conditions on the modulation frequency, which must be substantially higher than the reciprocal of the response time. Our experience suggests that a modulation frequency 30 to 100 times the response frequency gives satisfactory results.

By separating the ac and dc components of the electrical signals using circuits of known efficiency we can measure the AC/DC ratio in the original optical system.

9.3. SIGNAL-TO-NOISE IMPROVEMENT

9.3.1. Band Pass Filters

Because any transducer is liable to pick up noise, the ratio of signal to noise can be improved by the use of a filter tuned at or around the signal frequency. A filter tuned closely to the signal frequency is useful only if the modulation frequency can be held within narrow limits. It is also important to note that when phase measurement is required a narrowly tuned filter normally introduces phase shifts that alter rapidly if the modulation frequency drifts through the tuned frequency.

A fundamental requirement of any filter is that it should pass a band of frequencies wide enough to allow the output to vary at a rate corresponding to the required response time. If we define a response frequency as the reciprocal of the response time, the filter must pass the modulation frequency ± the response frequency. This suggests the use of a band pass filter.

A good deal of attention has been given to the design of band pass filters, but of late there has been a tendency to use active filters. These incorporate solid state amplifiers and have much better tuning characteristics than can be obtained with passive filters. The frequencies can be controlled closely by the adjustment of externally attached resistances.

In practice it is generally best to combine a low-pass and a high-pass filter in one stage of operation. By setting the low-pass filter to cut the high frequencies beyond the top of the band, and the high-pass filter to cut frequencies below the bottom of the band, any desired band can be set up. The "roll off" of a typical (Barr and Stroud) filter is 24 dB per octave, so that the band can be quite sharply defined.

When the modulation frequency is 30 times the response frequency, the band can be set at the modulation frequency ±3%. This gives a very useful suppression of noise. If the modulation frequency can be pushed up to 100 times the response frequency, a band of ±1% can be used with a correspondingly improved performance.

In the case of a modulation using a mechanically rotating element, such as a polarizer or halfwave plate, some allowance must be made for possible variations in rotational speed. In this case the band must be made wide enough for there to be a negligible fall of performance over a range controlled by the expected variation of speed. In the case of the Aston character reader, which uses an air turbine as a modulator, a band centered on 2500 Hz with ±300 Hz width has been found satisfactory. With care the turbine can be restarted to run at ±50 Hz of its previous speed, but the wider limits allow for some variation in air pressure.

9.3.2. The Homodyne Detector

A homodyne detector or lock-in amplifier is a phase-sensitive device which requires two inputs: the signal and a reference wave form of the same frequency. In principle, the two frequencies should be exactly the same and give a dc output signal whose magnitude is related to a mean level, being higher if the two inputs are in phase and lower if they are in antiphase.

In practice it is possible for the signal to have sidebands, so that the dc output varies relatively slowly. In other words, one can sample the signal for a time interval that can be built into the design. In a character reader this interval would correspond to the time the character was under the reading head. The operational frequency band of the amplifier must be designed accordingly.

The homodyne detector is an exceedingly powerful method of rejecting noise, since it can be readily arranged to pass the minimum frequency band required to operate the system. If the system is working slowly, for example, into a mechanical recorder with a time constant of several seconds and a slow chart speed, the bandpass is readily reduced to less than 1 Hz. In short, the bandpass automatically adjusts itself to that required to deliver the output.

The output of the homodyne is phase sensitive, as well as being amplitude sensitive. It is proportional to the projection of the signal complex amplitude vector onto the corresponding vector of the reference wave. Thus in situations where the phase is known to be constant, the homodyne can be used to measure the amplitude. If the amplitude is constant it will measure changes of phase, with an ambiguity as to whether the phase is in advance of the reference or lagging behind it. When both the amplitude and phase may vary, or where the phase is required unambiguously, it is necessary to use two homodyne detectors with the phases of their reference waves in quadrature.

Where the amplitude is known to vary and we only require a crude phase measurement (e.g., we want to know whether the signal is more nearly in phase with the reference than in antiphase), amplitude variations may be suppressed by clipping the signal by voltage clippers. As long as the signal is other than infinitesimal, the amplitude of the output is defined by the voltage clipper and it can then be compared with the reference signal similarly clipped. A homodyne detector then shows a rise or fall with respect to its mean level. Voltage clippers using biassed diodes have been used with success (Stephens 1971). Alternatively, one stage in the amplifier chain can be pushed to saturation giving a square-topped waveform of constant amplitude.

9.3.3. Homodyne Detectors in Phase-Related Pairs

If the reference or lock-in signal is split into two halves and one half is passed through a phase-shifting network to produce a signal in quadrature with the original, it is possible to use two homodyne detectors to determine unambiguously the amplitude and phase of the signal. The first homodyne measures the component of the signal amplitude projected onto the reference wave vector. The second homodyne gives the projection onto a vector at right angles to the reference wave. In this way, the real and imaginary parts of the signal can be measured independently. The technique was suggested for ionospheric holography in 1956 (Rogers 1956) but was not applied because of the difficulties of getting a Gabor and Goss interferometer to recombine the outputs (Gabor and Goss 1966).

Although the two components of the signal give, in principle, the whole output they may not give a convenient measure. Thus if the modulus is required, the components must be squared, added, and square rooted. Analogue circuits to achieve this calculation are very difficult to devise. The signal can be digitized, but there is still some computation to be done. However, if it is required to detect the phase, the first step is to divide one signal by the other to give tan ψ. There is then a further ambiguity in that a positive tan ψ only indicates that ψ is in the first *or* third quadrant, and the signs of the components must be inspected to obtain an exact answer.

It should also be noted that the output from a homodyne detector appears as a departure from a mean level corresponding to zero signal input. Care is needed to keep this mean level steady. Then it must be subtracted from the actual output before either analogue or digital work can proceed.

The most favorable case is that of measurement or machine tool control, where the property of interest is the phase. This is particularly the case in moire pattern applications, since an accurate determination of phase is equivalent to subdividing the fringe number, or the interval of the moire pattern grating. In this case, we have the additional advantage that the amplitude of the signal is reasonably constant. If the

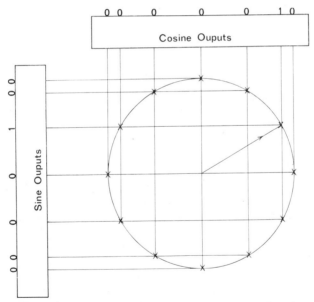

Figure 9.1 Logic circuit for digitized phase output from two Homodyne detectors. Above, digitized output from cosine phased detector. This gives an output 1 corresponding to the nearest voltage step to present output and 0 elsewhere. Left-hand side. Similar outputs from sine phased detector. In circle, "AND" gates driving indicator lamps. Constant amplitude is assumed as in a moire pattern displacement indicator. The presence of a cosine output 0000010 and a sine output 0000100 indicates a phase of 30°, and the 30° lamp lights up.

two outputs are suitably digitized, it is possible to devise a logical network (Figure 9.1) that will yield a digital output, either in fractions of a fringe or in equivalent steps of circular measure. With a Peek rotator (Peek et al. 1969) where there is a small degree of nonuniformity in the output, steps of 20° are quite safe and 10° are possible. Again the extent of fringe subdivision depends on the integrating time available and on the steadiness of the amplitude. If the amplitude is varying slightly as well as the phase, the digitizing points will have to be set for an average amplitude and there may be slight errors in their triggering, with uncertainty in the indicated phase angle.

9.4. THE REFERENCE SIGNAL

There are basically two types of reference signal: the type derived from an electrical drive, and a signal derived from a parallel channel by optical or magnetic impulses.

9.4.1. Reference Signals from the Electrical Drive

In a number of applications where the temporal modulation is achieved by electrical means, a fraction of the drive voltage may be divided off to give a reference signal. Examples would be the piezoelectrically driven interferometer of Kozma and Massey (1969), or the electro-optic modulators or rotators such as used by Macovski (1968) which are available from the Malvern Instrument Company. In the case of sinusoidal modulation the voltage may be divided and applied to the homodyne detector, but if the modulator produces a Bessel function series, it may be necessary to frequency multiply the modulating signal so as to isolate the required harmonic of the drive. Since the drive frequency is at least nominally fixed this creates no difficulty.

In the case of the saw-toothed drive associated with the electro-optic rotator, the wave form has to be modified. Again the frequency is nominally fixed, so that a filter can be used to isolate the fundamental. The higher harmonics can be cut with a low-pass filter, and this will give an output that is closely sinusoidal.

9.4.2. Reference Signals Indirectly Obtained

In systems involving mechanical rotation an indirect method is recommended. The chief application is to the case where the modulator is spun in an air turbine. Here, the rotational speed is dependent on the air pressure, and, although properly designed control gear can hold this within close limits, there is always some uncertainty as to the speed. The same applies to induction motors, where the small degree of "slip" between the speed and the drive frequency makes it necessary to derive a signal from the rotator.

A possible way to derive the signal is to put a white spot on the edge of the rotator and observe its passage past a fixed point with a photodiode. Another scheme, which is used by Barr and Stroud on their rotating prismatic Q-switch, is to attach a small magnet to the rotator and use a sensing coil. In both cases, some care is required in the design to secure a reasonably sinusoidal output. The Q-switch, for instance, produces a relatively short pulse, which is suitable for the synchronous triggering of the flash tube.

In the case of the rotating polarizer or halfwave plate, it is best simply to use a parallel channel to give the basic frequency. A fixed polarizer followed by a pinhead diode will give the correct frequency for the rotator, and phase relative to the rotation is preset by adjusting the angle of the fixed polarizer relative to the apparatus.

Where it is desired to use two homodyne detectors in quadrature, the two reference signals can be derived from two pinhead diodes, with polarizers set at 45° to one another. This avoids any problems with conventional phase shifting networks, which tend to vary a little if the frequency drifts.

In addition to the use of a polarizer in an air turbine, there have recently been developed electric motors with hollow shafts which can be spun at 60,000 rpm with a high-frequency drive. Starting as induction motors, these motors achieve synchronous speed. In principle, a reference signal can now be obtained from the drive power supply. This, of course, not only assumes zero slip but presupposes that the phase relation between the drive and the rotor will always reset to the same angle whenever the motor is restarted. So far we have no data on this aspect of their performance.

9.4.3. Use of the Reference Signal to Give the dc Level and for Normalization

In some applications, especially character recognition, the reference signal is essentially the signal for zero spatial frequency; that is, it gives the integrated intensity of the input. This, therefore, corresponds to the DC level of the illumination. Consequently, we can use the corresponding dc electrical level for AC/DC comparisons. The ac channels derived from the various AC spatial frequencies are now required to pass only the ac signal. It is not necessary to split the AC channels to give both ac and dc levels, since the dc level can be obtained from the reference channel.

Similarly the dc level from the reference channel can be used for normalization. If the intensity of the light source shows a long-term drift, this will affect the dc level on the reference channel to the same extent as it affects the ac level on the spatial frequency channel. If the AC/DC comparison is now obtained by "backing off" the ac and dc terms, normalization is achieved.

9.5. THE AC/DC RATIO: RECTIFIER NETWORKS

When it is necessary to make a comparison between the AC and DC elements in the optical spatial frequency by comparing the ac and dc terms, the dc term can readily be isolated as a voltage by the use of a low-pass filter designed to eliminate the ac term.

To complete the comparison, the ac term must be reduced to a dc voltage proportional to the r.m.s. value of the ac term. There are a number of ways of doing this

1. Use of a homodyne circuit
2. Use of two homodyne circuits in quadrature
3. Use of a rectifier network

The first method is phase sensitive and gives strictly the component of the ac signal in phase with the reference wave. The second method is also phase sensitive; but the two outputs can be combined to give the modulus of the ac original and hence its r.m.s. value. As we have seen this calculation of the modulus requires specially designed circuits, which are not easy to control.

The third alternative is relatively simple to set up, but has the real disadvantage that the dc voltage generated represents the sum of all the ac components, of whatever frequency, that arise in the apparatus. The performance of the device is, therefore, liable to be very erratic unless care is taken to use a narrow band pass filter to remove all unwanted frequencies. High-frequency "mush" is particularly troublesome.

In our laboratory, we often use this third system. After careful filtering, the input signal is amplified and applied to the primary of an interstage transformer. This has the useful effect of isolating the secondary, with its Wheatstone bridge rectified circuit, completely from the amplifiers. This in turn ensures that the original dc term cannot get through, though the narrow band pass filter normally deals with this. It also means that either end of the rectifier can be earthed according to requirements. If desired, a high-resistance potential divider can be put across the rectifier output and any intermediate point earthed.

This flexibility is of great use in applications where "backing off" is used. In the normalization technique referred to in Section 9.4.3, we can earth one end of the bridge rectifier on the reference signal amplifier, and the other end of the bridge rectifier on the signal amplifier. Thus the reference signal produces, say, a positive voltage, and the signal amplifier produces a negative voltage. These two voltages are then tied to the ends of a potential divider, and the voltage of an intermediate point is compared with earth on a comparator or Schmidt trigger. By adjusting the intermediate point, the ratio of signal to reference that will switch the Schmidt trigger may be preset. Once this is done, the system is automatically normalized against light fluctuations, since proportional changes in the signal and reference analogue voltages leave the switching point of the potential divider unchanged.

In spite of the tendency of rectifier circuits to integrate over a wide frequency band, we have found them very satisfactory when combined with a narrow band pass filter.

9.6. HETERODYNING

Once a signal has been obtained in the form of an ac electrical signal of known frequency ω_1, it is possible to mix it with a frequency ω_2, derived from a local oscillator, in a nonlinear electrical circuit. This will give rise to two extra outputs at frequencies $(\omega_1 - \omega_2)$ and $(\omega_1 + \omega_2)$. If the values of ω_1 and ω_2 are correctly chosen, it is possible to isolate either of the two combination frequencies by the use of a tuned or band pass filter. For example, a complete frequency analysis of a given input signal can be made by varying ω_2 and passing the sum frequency $(\omega_1 + \omega_2)$ through a very sharply tuned fixed frequency filter; for example, one containing a quartz crystal. The output at $(\omega_1 + \omega_2)$ which is a fixed frequency P, will give the magnitude of the frequency ω_1 in the system. By slowly varying ω_2, one can explore the frequencies over a range from $\omega_1 = P$ to $\omega_1 = 0$ when $\omega_2 = P$.

The system will also work on the difference frequency $(\omega_1 - \omega_2)$ and it must be borne in mind that if $(\omega_1 - \omega_2) = P$, an ambiguity will arise in the interpretation of the output curve. This can be avoided by restricting the range of ω_1 to $0 \rightarrow P/2$ and thus restricting the range of ω_2 to $P/2 \rightarrow P$.

Heterodyning can be used for a number of purposes

1. Reducing an unacceptable high ω_1 to a difference frequency $(\omega_1 - \omega_2)$ which is lower. An example of this occurs in the work of Macovski (1968) discussed in Section 8.4.4.

2. Increasing the frequency of a signal, so as to improve the smoothing performance of a rectifier network (Paragraph 9.5).

3. Separation of a number of frequencies in a multifrequency system, along the general lines given above.

9.7. MULTIFREQUENCY SYSTEMS

There are a number of multifrequency systems and they vary in their properties. The original character reader of Leifer, Rogers, and Stephens (1969) using a wobbly mirror (Section 8.4.3) produced a signal that was not a pure tone, and moreover its mean ac frequency was a function of the optical AC frequency. Thus the electronic processing of the system is assisted because the various channels have different mean frequencies so band pass filters can be used to improve the signal-to-noise ratio.

The main multifrequency systems are, however, based on a combination of pure tones, and these may be separated by a set of filters, or by heterodyning into a fixed filter. The pure tones are normally generated in some temporal modulation device which allows a reference signal to be generated. The use of a set of homodyne detectors therefore suggests itself as a means of signal separation.

An important problem centers on the choice of the frequencies to be used on the various modulators. Thus if we choose a set $\omega_1, \omega_2, \omega_3, \ldots, -\omega_i, \omega_j \ldots \omega_n$ it has to be borne in mind that not only will these frequencies exist, but as soon as they are applied to a nonlinear system such as a detector, all frequencies $(\omega_i - \omega_j)$ $(i \neq j)$ appear as well. Some care is necessary to avoid overlapping and ambiguity in this assembly of $\frac{1}{2}n(n-1)$ combination frequencies.

A useful starting point is a Leech series (Leech 1955). This is a series of numbers or of intervals, such that their *differences* represent the numbers $1, 2, 3, \ldots, N$. There are two types of series, a restricted series where no number greater than N occurs, and an unrestricted series which contains numbers greater than N as well as all the numbers 1 to N. Either series is suitable for our purposes.

Many of these series have multiple solutions; for example, the number 8 can be obtained in more than one way. This could be inconvenient, although it is generally possible to choose the frequencies so that each can be isolated with ease without using a redundant value. Of greater importance is the fact that all the beat frequencies, while distinct, nevertheless lie on a harmonic series, so that higher harmonics of the fundamental can be confused with higher frequencies detected in their fundamental mode.

A good deal can be done to reduce these difficulties by modifying a Leech series. The Leech series is essentially a set of integers, and is, therefore, useful in the design of partially coherent filters (Davies and Rogers 1977). The set of modulation frequencies do not need to be integral multiples of the smaller difference, so that individual frequencies may be set a nonintegral amount high or low on the ideal Leech series, whereby a satisfactory and nonoverlapping set of combination frequencies can be obtained. The set of frequencies will also differ from a set of harmonics.

9.8. DIGITIZATION AND LOGIC CIRCUITS

Many of the processes for handling optical signals result in an analogue dc voltage. Thus the homodyne detector has a dc output and so has the rectifier system. Analog signals are not easy to handle, and hence it is usual to digitize them to give a result in binary numbers. Thus the first character reader described by Leifer et al. (1969), digitized the analogue voltages in a set of eight steps, corresponding to a three-bit binary number. This was done on three channels. The phase term on one channel was also digitized to give a one-bit binary output corresponding to + or − of phase.

Many devices for this purpose are described in the literature. The modern digital voltmeter uses a ramp generator and comparator to stop a counter as soon as the ramp voltage reaches the external voltage. Leifer et al. (1969) used a potential divider, and various steps on this were connected to comparators, which therefore switched in sequence as the analogue voltage increased. A simple Boolean logic circuit then converts the steps to a three-bit binary number (Stephens 1971). Many other variations are possible.

In the case of the normalizer procedure of Section 9.5, we can produce a number of steps by running a set of potential dividers in parallel across the outputs from the reference and signal bridge rectifiers. By setting the intermediate point at various ratios on the successive potential dividers, the associated comparators can be made to switch in sequence.

More or less conventional Boolean logic circuits can be devised for operations such as character recognition. A number of channels are run in parallel, and, in general, these switch a larger number of comparators. By using a set of comparators with a built-in inverter that produces either on or off outputs at different points, it is possible to build up a decision circuit. It is necessary to use a large AND gate for each symbol to be recognized; each gate is then connected to comparators relevant to such a decision. The AND gate is connected in a way that enables one to choose the positive output or the inverse output according to whether that comparator should be on or off in its positive phase to give an output corresponding to the symbol. A diagram illustrating this is given in Figure 9.2.

Another useful device addresses itself to the question of separating one character from the next. In this case the character string is passed across a vertical line of photodetectors at a known rate. The output of the detectors now goes to a shift register clocked so that the output travels down the shift register. A logic circuit tests for continuity and when this fails the content of the shift register is dumped into a store, and the shift register now begins to build up the next character. The circuitry is rather complex and is described in Rogers and Stephens (1973).

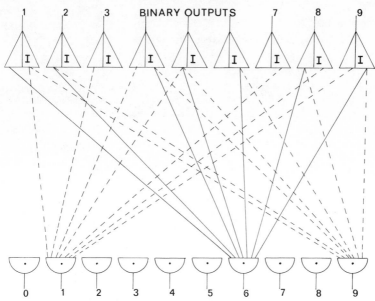

Figure 9.2 Logic circuit for character recognition. Above, 9 binary outputs connected to inverters (in practice comparators will give both direct and inverse outputs). Below, 10 "AND" gates are used to indicate the letter under the reading head. Binary output 1 is a phase output. Outputs 2 and 3 correspond to a single spatial frequency split at two voltage levels V_1 and V_2. Thus if $V < V_1$, $2 = 0$, if $V > V_1$, $2 = 1$. While if $V < V_2$, $3 = 0$ and if $V > V_2$, $3 = 1$. 6 and 7 are similar. The number 6 under the reading head gives rise to outputs $11 \cdot 010 \cdot 10$, where the dot indicates that 6 is indifferent to outputs 3 and 7. Thus as long as $V > V_1$, it is unimportant whether $V > V_2$ or not. 6 will only indicate if the AND gate 6 has all 1's on its input lines. It is, therefore, connected as shown, collecting 1's from the direct side of the inverters where binary output 1 is expected and from the inverted side of the invertors where binary 0 is expected. Inverters to which the output is indifferent are not connected. Dotted lines show connections to 1 that correspond to an output $0 \cdot 111 \cdot 001$, while 9 is connected to the output $01 \cdot 010 \cdot 10$. Note that since 6 and 9 have inversion symmetry, they are distinguished by the phase channel 1 only.

REFERENCES

Davies, J. C. and G. L. Rogers (1977). *Opt. Commun.* **21** (2) 311–317.

Gabor, D. and W. Goss (1966). *J. Opt. Soc. Amer.* **56**, 849–858.

Kozma, A. and N. Massey (1969). *Appl. Opt.* **8**, 393–397.

Leech, J., (1955). *Proc. Math. Soc. London* **32**, 169.

Leifer, I., G. L. Rogers, and N. W. F. Stephens (1969) *Opt. Acta* **16**, 535–553.

Macovski, A. (1968). Ph.D. Thesis. "Efficient holography using temporal modulation." Stanford University, Stanford, Calif.

Peek, T., H. de Lang, and G. Bouwhuis (1969). *Laser and Opto-Electronics Conference,* Southampton. S117.

Phelan, R. J. and A. R. Cook (1973). *Appl. Opt.* **12**, 2494.

Rogers, G. L. (1956). *Nature (GB)* **177**, 613–614.

Rogers, G. L. and N. W. F. Stephens (1973). B. P. 1,311,671.

Stephens, N. W. F. (1971). Ph.D. Thesis. "Character recognition systems using Fourier transformation in incoherent light". University of Aston, Birmingham, England.

10

Examples of
Noncoherent Processing

There are a number of applications of noncoherent processes in various
states of development. They employ a number of the devices described
in earlier chapters, in various combinations. Some, such as optical
transfer function (O.T.F.) machines, use temporal modulation but not
parallel processing. Others, such as reading machines that compare the
input characters with a set of analysis masks, use parallel processing but
not temporal modulation. Other systems, such as the scheme for
increasing photographic speed with a lenticular grid, use spatial modulation. We consider first a system that combines a large number of
techniques, except spatial modulation, which is known as the Aston
Character Reader.

10.1. THE ASTON CHARACTER READER

This system of character recognition embodies a combination of the
above principles. We start with a noncoherently illuminated character.
This means we can use ordinary light to illuminate, and the characters
can be printed on a diffuse background. The character can be black on
white or white on black. So far most of the work has been done with the
latter. The use of a black on white input means that we start with a DC
bias under circumstances where it is not necessary. It also means that
special care must be used to apodize the edge of the field to ensure that
the frame does not add a constant set of frequencies over and above those
sought in the character.

The character is analyzed for spatial frequencies by setting it up as the input of a spatial frequency filter (Figure 4.3). In order to obtain data on a finite number of frequencies, we run a number of spatial frequency filters side by side with a common input in a parallel processing system.

To obtain an electrical output for each frequency, we use temporal modulation. In the earliest model the modulator was a wobbly mirror, but this is incapable of high-frequency operation. In the preferred system, therefore, we use an optical selsyn activated by a rotating polarizer or halfwave plate spun in an air turbine. Other means of rotation could be employed but many of them require the light to be traveling in a collimated beam. The rotating plate will work over an angle of 20°, which enables parallel processing to be used.

The inclusion of the optical selsyn means we are using the principle of sequential switching, and it gives an ac output that represents in amplitude and phase the corresponding AC spatial frequency in the character. The zero of phase is obtained by the use of a pin diode viewing the letter directly through a fixed polarizer. This also gives a measure of the average flux of light from the character—the zero spatial frequency terms. The principles of the electronics are given in Chapter 9. By making electronic phase comparisons, it is possible to distinguish inverted characters such as 6 and 9. Finally, electronic logic circuits are used to make the decisions.

Figure 10.1 gives a sketch of the system. The input is shown on the left. This may be a printed sheet, but in preliminary work characters on a 16 mm film were passed through a camera diffusely illuminated from behind. The rotating polarizer is placed close in front of the character to give as wide a cone of light as possible. Within this cone, analysis grids G_1 and G_2 are set up, each with a clear region in the center of the cone. The average DC level and the phase comparison term is obtained from this central beam falling on a pinhead diode D behind a polarizer P.

The grid G_1 is split up into four zones, each carrying a particular spatial frequency. This grid acts as the shadowing grid or middle element in the spatial frequency filter. The grid G_2 carries four composite grids, each of which is split up into three phase-shifted regions in the manner of Figure 8.11. The two grids G_1 and G_2 are shown in Figure 10.2a and b. The triple regions on G_2 are provided with polarizers at 60° orientation and detection is by a set of four solar cells S, shown schematically as S_1 and S_2 in Figure 10.1. Balance is obtained by shifting S_1 and S_2 sideways in a special mount, so that there is no ac output when no shadow is

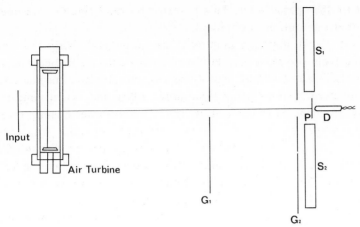

Figure 10.1 Section through Aston character reader. Left, input character. Next air turbine with rotating polarizer (or fixed polarizer, not shown, and rotating halfwave plate). G_1 = multichannel shadowing grid, G_2 = phase split grid corresponding to G_1 (see Figure 10.2), S_1, S_2 = solar cells, P = polarizer, D = pinhead diode. The straight-through beam passes through central holes in G_1 and G_2 to give a phase reference and normalizing beam.

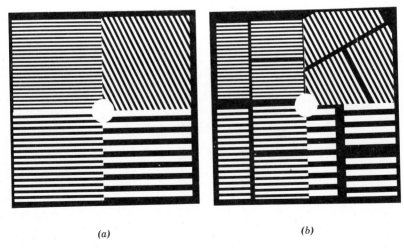

(a) (b)

Figure 10.2 Photographs of grids (a) G_1 and (b) G_2. The central hole is clearly visible. The phase reference and normalizing beam pass straight through these holes. In use G_2 is reproduced on a larger scale to allow for projective magnification.

found by the spatial filter. This is tested by removing G_1 and checking that a zero ac output is obtained.

The spatial frequencies employed are, in general, fairly low and are selected from the plots of relative efficiency calculated theoretically by Leifer (Leifer et al. 1969). This system is, therefore, in marked contrast with coherent systems using Fraunhofer diffraction, which tend to lose the low frequencies in the scatter from the zero-order beam. Moreover, the Fraunhofer systems only work from a photographic transparency.

The electrical signals from the solar cells are passed through narrow band pass filters, amplified and rectified as described in Section 9.5. The comparison signal from the photodiode D is used to give a phase zero and also to normalize the system against light fluctuations. The analogue output voltages are made to actuate comparators that give binary signals in the manner discussed in Section 9.6. These are finally passed into a logic circuit as indicated in Section 9.8. A fuller account has been given by Stephens (1971).

So far work has been limited to a system using a cinefilm input with 10 characters, the Arabic numerals $0, 1, \ldots, 9$. The design reading rate is 30–100 characters a second and the output is on a standard five-hole punch. By making a film loop, a given set of characters can be presented

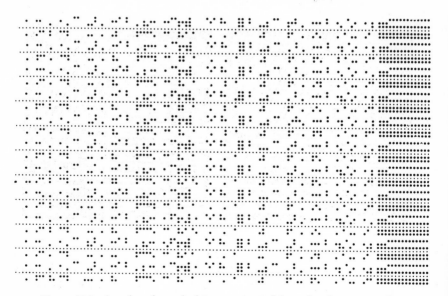

Figure 10.3 A series of punched tapes outputted from the character reader.

repetitively a large number of times, and the reliability of the system can be tested.

Use of a limited five-bit output fed directly into a punch without decoding has enjoyed a measure of success (Rogers 1974) (Figure 10.3), but finer subdivision of the voltage levels will be required. This alteration has been started, but the project has been delayed by a cutback in university funding.

10.2. O.T.F. MEASUREMENT

The Scientific Instrument Research Association (S.I.R.A.) has produced a machine (Baker 1965) that measures the optical transfer function of a lens both on axis and for tangential and sagital sections off axis. The input consists of a slit, crossed with a spatial frequency. The pattern moves sideways at a constant temporal frequency of the order of 1 kHz. In practice this is achieved by using an annular track on a radial grating spun about its center. The angle between the slit and the lines on the radial grating can be varied (Figure 10.4) so that the effective spatial frequency can be varied.

The lens forms an image of the slit and the corresponding system of

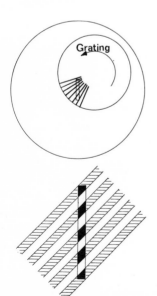

Figure 10.4 Diagram of the object used in the Sira O.T.F. measuring machine. A rotating grating generates an object by movement behind a slit at an angle θ, which can be varied to alter the input spatial frequency. The motion produces temporal modulation of the phase.

black and white stripes in the conjugate plane. This image is received on another narrow slit at right angles to the image line and the signal passing through the slit falls on a photomultiplier. If the lens is forming a good image, the passage of the black and white stripes across the photomultiplier slit gives rise to a strong ac signal. This ac signal takes the form of a square-topped wave with equal black and white regions, which means that the average dc level corresponds to half the peak or "on" part of the cycle.

If the image produced by the lens lacks contrast, the average dc level remains roughly constant but the ac ripple is progressively reduced. The optical transfer function is defined as the percentage ripple relative to the maximum black and white signal. This in itself measures the modulation transfer function, which is sufficient for many purposes.

The optical transfer function itself is a complex number and so far we have only measured its modulus. It is necessary also to measure its phase, for which a reference signal is required. A small fraction of the light from the source is, therefore, split off by a beam splitting prism (Figure 10.5) and focused on a local photomultiplier; the signal is

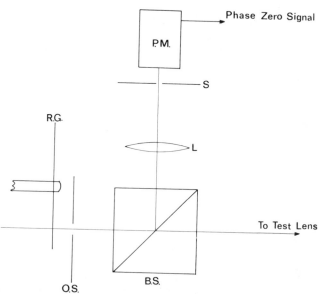

Figure 10.5 Diagram of source system in Sira O.T.F. machine. R.G. = Rotating grid, O.S. = object slit, B.S. = beam splitter, S = a slit or pinhole conjugate with OS in BS and the lens L, P.M. = the photomultiplier which gives the phase reference signal.

separated by a slit or pinhole to generate the ac reference signal. This signal is compared electronically with the phase of the signal derived from the image plane detector.

Both the ac and phase outputs are recorded on a chart recorder. During the progress of the chart the angle between the object slit and the radial grating (Figure 10.4) is gradually altered. Starting with the radial grating parallel to the object strip, we get temporal modulation from black to white, but the spatial frequency *along* the slit is zero. It is generally assumed the O.T.F. of the lens is 100% at zero frequency and its phase error in zero. This thus allows the chart to be set up to start from a fixed point. As the angle between the radial grating and slit increases so does the spatial frequency, and in general the O.T.F. falls and its phase may change. The spatial frequency reaches a maximum, set by the radial grating, when the lines on the latter are perpendicular to the object slit.

If it is desired to proceed to higher spatial frequencies, a special relay lens is added to the system to produce an aerial image of the object system on a reduced scale. The design of this system requires some care, as the object should be noncoherent. The imaging of small systems at a finite distance with a lens of finite aperture is liable to produce partial coherence effects.

As far as I know no work has been done measuring O.T.F. with various directions of polarization. Using a lens off axis is liable to introduce polarization effects owing to the oblique passage of the light through the surfaces, and in extreme cases this could be quite noticeable.

It will be seen that the O.T.F. machine uses temporal modulation and electronic processing but not parallel processing. The cost of the input and output systems is so high that it would be impractical to duplicate them, though theoretically one can put two light beams through the lens at different angles simultaneously. With the very expensive phase reference source, multiple images could be formed by mirrors when the relatively cheap detectors could be duplicated in the image plane. Care would have to be taken to calibrate the mirrors.

10.3. PRINT REGISTRATION AND RELATED SYSTEMS

Work at Sira has developed the use of the basic input device to modulate light falling on a moving object to monitor its movement.

Several applications of this device have been made by West (West 1971). It has been successfully used to check the registration of printed material as it moves past the head; error signals produced can then be fed back into the system. Multiple detectors with color filters can be used to monitor color balance. Similar techniques are also available for checking microcircuits.

10.4. DETECTION OF MOTION BY A NONCONTACT METHOD

The use of moire patterns to monitor machine tools is well known, and in conventional systems it involves the movement of two fine gratings, perhaps a meter or more long, accurately parallel to themselves with their surfaces separated by 0.05 mm or less. This calls for great

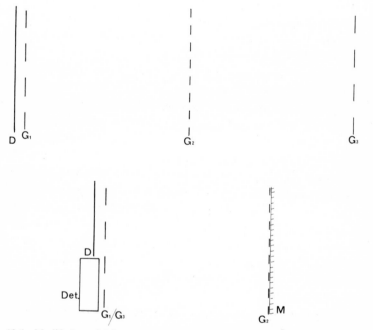

Figure 10.6   Modified spatial frequency filter for noncontact moire work. (*a*) conventional filter based on Figure 4.3 but drawn symmetrically. D = diffuse source, G₁, G₂, and G₃ = filter grids. (*b*) Folded filter using mirror M. D is now off axis and the other half of the input plane carries the detector. The same grid now acts both for G_1 and G_3. G_2 is placed in contact with the mirror.

mechanical perfection, and a small piece of dirt accidentally entering the space between the rulings can seriously damage the surfaces.

Pettigrew has developed a variation of the spatial frequency filter (Figure 4.3) that results in a system capable of working with a separation of 30 cm or more (Pettigrew 1974). In the coarse grating version, which operates by geometrical optics, the spatial frequency filter of Figure 4.3 is folded up. The central grating, which is half the spacing or twice the frequency of the two outer ones, is formed on a mirror. The output grating is then imaged on the input grating by the mirror, and the laws of reflection ensure that the correspondence is exact whatever the distance from input to mirror (subject to the absence of diffraction) (Figure 10.6). A slight angle between the lines of the input and mirror gratings will give visible moire fringes, which may be counted either visually or with a photodetector. This system will work over 30 cm so that the input grating can be well separated from the moving part.

Pettigrew has further discovered that the system will work in the diffractive region, only here all three gratings must be the same size. The system now resembles a folded Marton interferometer (Marton 1952, 1953). By the use of fine gratings very small movements can be detected and the problems of small clearances altogether overcome.

10.5. USE OF LENTICULAR SCREENS

10.5.1. Pulse Width Modulation

It is possible to obtain lenticular screens such as are used for stereoscopic photography and on "3-D" postcards. These are gratings consisting of a series of cylindrical lenses placed side by side with a spacing of typically 0.3–0.5 mm. They are normally molded or embossed on a plastic base.

These screens lend themselves to experiments on spatial modulation. A student project experiment by Jacobs (unpublished) made use of this system. A triangular diffuse source is set up in front of a lenticular screen, which, by the cylindrical lens effect mentioned in Chapter 1, forms a triangular repeated variation of intensity in the common focal plane of the screen (Figure 10.7). If this light now falls on a high-contrast plate, such that the peak intensity fogs it entirely and the trough intensity fails to act on it at all, a black and white grating will result. The

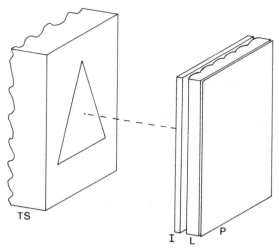

Figure 10.7 Apparatus of Jacobs for producing a pulse width modulated picture. TS = triangular source, I = input negative, L = lenticular screen, P = photographic plate.

exact point where the plate "switches" will be a function of exposure: if the exposure is low only a narrow region around the peak will switch. If it is high, all but the trough will go black (Figure 10.8).

If now a negative or image is placed in contact with or projected onto the front of the lenticular screen, different places will have different exposures. The period of the grating formed will be constant, given by the lenticular spacing, but its black to white ratio will vary all over the picture. A representation of the scene is thus produced, no point of which is other than all black or all white. This is the principle and mode of action of the halftone screen, which is operated with screens in two dimensions (Ives 1899). The method has also been used to produce a modulated grating (Rogers 1970).

Jacobs superimposed pictures on screens as above, and then combined them so that two pictures occurred on one plate with their carrier frequencies at right angles. With this method, coherent optical processing allows a degree of separation. Theory shows that there will be a degree of "cross talk," but this can be much reduced by reducing the depth of modulation of each picture. Recovery in the first-order spectrum of the carrier is now of low contrast, but this can be offset by basing the recovered image on, say, the third order of diffraction. Owing to the limited time of a student project, Jacobs did not explore the latter possibility fully, but his results in the first order showed a useful degree of separation. The system is an example of a "hybrid" system.

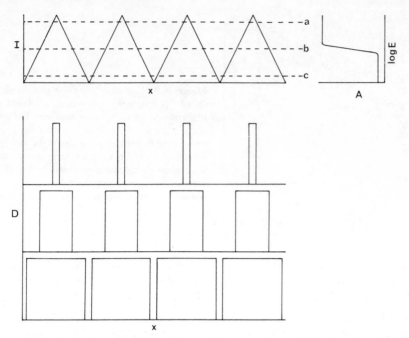

Figure 10.8 Production of a pulse width modulated negative. Above, intensity distance plot produced by Figure 10.7 in the absence of an input negative. a, b, c = Possible exposure levels corresponding to the switch level of the plate characteristics (top right). Exposure a < b < c. Below, the black pulses produced when the exposure causes switching at levels a, b, and c, respectively.

By altering the balance between the two pictures, there is a distinct possibility of producing an output which gives a normal impression of an ordinary picture on one carrier, but nevertheless contains a recoverable second picture on the other carrier at a much weaker level.

10.5.2. High-Speed Photography

One of the problems of high speed photography is that by using a fast wide aperture lens one loses focal depth, while by stopping down one loses photographic speed. It is possible to use a lenticular screen to achieve a useful compromise.

Suppose you stop down your lens and place a lenticular screen immediately in front of your plate. Although the direct light may be quite insufficient to record on the plate, the lenticular screen concentrates it onto a narrow strip in the center of each lenticulation (Figure

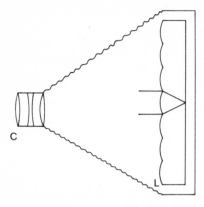

Figure 10.9 Use of a lenticular grid in high-speed photography. C = camera lens of moderate to small relative aperture, L = lenticular plate greatly enlarged. Rays from C appear sensibly parallel on scale of the enlargement and focus on a narrow strip in the back focal plane giving enhanced photographic effect locally. The negative must be coherently processed to recover the image at adequate contrast.

10.9). With a really good lenticular screen the concentration of light could be sixtyfold. This is roughly equivalent to increasing the F/number of your taking lens eight-fold. In this way you could obtain the focal depth of an F/32 lens, together with the speed of an F/4 lens, or any similar combination. An increase in the aperture of the taking lens beyond a certain point does not increase the speed, because it simply increases the region in the back focal plane over which the light is spread. Further progress can be made by using two lenticular grids crossed to form a "fly's eye" type of network. In the limit, the speed is given by the F/number of the lenticular grid and the focal depth by the F/number of the taking lens.

The photographic record produced is in itself quite indistinguishable to the naked eye from a completely unexposed plate, since the black region obstructs negligible light. The picture is, however, securely coded on a carrier frequency and can be recovered by coherent processing in the first-order spectrum. To reduce the exposure time, one can decode by allowing all the nonzero spectra to pass, although the carrier frequency will now appear on the output. For this reason, the system is a "hybrid" system.

Devices of this kind were in use before World War II, but they have now been superceded by holography, which allows objects at different distances to be recovered successively during reconstruction. Because of the relatively low speed of holographic plates, there may yet be a small region of very difficult photography where these devices could be used with high-speed plates.

10.5.3. High-Speed Motion Photography

Courtney-Pratt (1953, 1966) has developed an ingenious system of motion photography using a large aperture lens with a scanning disk spinning rapidly in front of it and crossed lenticular screens in the image plane (Figure 10.10). An ordinary lens has redundancy, because it parallel processes a number of input directions from the object. This is shown in the old color process using lenticular screens (Figure 1.3). Courtney-Pratt uses this parallel processing facility to achieve time resolution, allowing the various directional bundles into the lens successively through the spinning disk. The bundles are then kept separate by the lenticular array, which addresses each signal to a different point in the focal plane of the lenticulations. It is enormously more complex than the color process, which has only three addresses; in a good system one can have 10^3–10^4 addresses.

Just as the color picture is recovered by projection back through the system, so various shots in the time sequence can be recovered by projecting back through the lens system, with the scanning disk taking different positions successively. A very slow rotation of the scanning disk gives a replay of the motion of the object at a correspondingly decreased speed.

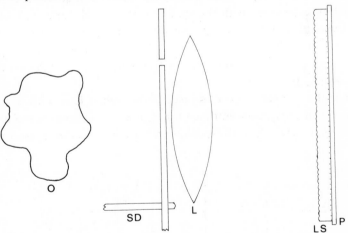

Figure 10.10 High-speed "image dissecting" camera of Courtney-Pratt. O = object, S.D. = scanning disk, L = lens imaging O onto plate, L.S. = a two-dimensional lenticular screen normally produced by crossing two cylindrical screens, P = plate. The image is recovered by projecting backwards through the system (reversibility of rays, compare with Figure 1.3).

10.6. NONCOHERENT DEBLURRING

There is a considerable body of work on deblurring photographs by coherent processes using filters in the Fraunhofer plane of a coherent system. The technique is potentially very powerful; however, it requires an input transparency, and coherent techniques are notoriously vulnerable to noise. It is particularly easy to get a restored image considerably distorted by "ringing" at the sharp edges.

Although deblurring is normally discussed in terms of Fourier transforms and convolution, the basic idea is that blurring reduces the higher spatial frequencies in the object, and these must be restored by selective amplification. In the case of a square-topped linear blur, deblurring is complicated by zeros and phase inversion. In the case of a Gaussian linear blur this complication does not arise—the progressive loss of high frequencies can be restored by a progressive amplification of them.

To avoid using coherent objects, we can illuminate our blurred picture with quasi-monochromatic light. The picture does not need to be a transparency, it can be a print. We now image it with a lens using an entrance pupil filter (Armitage and Lohmann 1965; Burch and Forno 1975; Rogers and Davies 1977). In this case the pupil is a compromise devised by Davies to simulate a Gaussian correction curve. It consists of a set of slits arranged with the spacings of a Leech series (Leech 1955), but of variable height. The extreme slits pass the highest frequencies and are therefore taller than the others. There is some redundancy in the system as the light slits generate 28 frequencies, of which two or three are redundant.

When the blurred object is imaged through a lens with a correctly scaled set of slits in its entrance pupil, there is an enhancement of the higher frequencies. Strictly speaking we are now in the region of partial

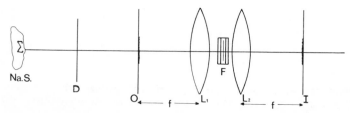

Figure 10.11 Apparatus for noncoherent deblurring. Na.S. = monochromatic source, D = diffuser, O = blurred input object, L_1, L_2 = lenses (one is in principle sufficient), F = filter in liquid gate, I = deblurred image.

coherence (Appendix V). The requisite exposure tends to be rather long, but the results show a distinct improvement particularly in edge sharpness. The apparatus is shown in Figure 10.11.

The input object was made from Figure 10.12, using the cylindrical lens technique (Chapter 1) to convert the variable area diagram of Figure 10.12 into a variable density record. This was then photographed in the apparatus of Figure 10.11 using the entrance pupil filter of Figure 10.13.

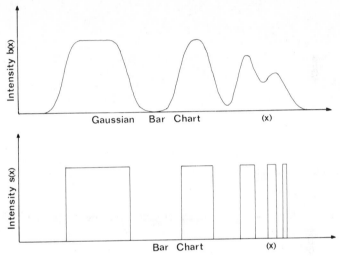

Figure 10.12 Photo of input (*a*) blurred and (*b*) sharp. These were painted around and photographed through a cylindrical lens.

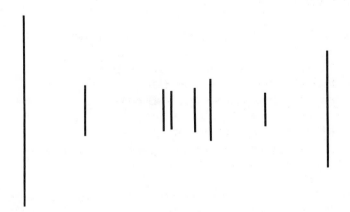

Fig. 10.13 The deblurring filter.

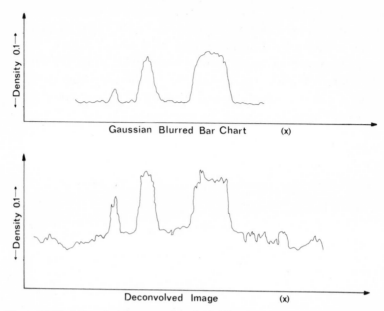

Figure 10.14   Microphotometer traces of (*a*) blurred image and (*b*) recovered image.

Figure 10.14 shows microphotometer traces of the corrected and uncorrected signals. It is of interest that this technique is much less likely to produce noise artifacts or ringing than a purely coherent technique.

REFERENCES

Armitage, J. D. and A. W. Lohmann (1965). *Appl. Opt.* **4**, 461–467.

Baker, L. R. (1965). *Jap. J. Appl. Phys.* **4**, suppl. 1, 146–152.

Burch, J. M., and C. Forno (1975). *Opt. Eng.* **14**, 178–185.

Courtney-Pratt, J. S., (1953). *J. Photog. Sci.* **1**, 21.

Courtney-Pratt, J. S. (1966). *Rev. Sci. Inst.* **37**, 1364–1366.

Ives, F. E. (1899) *Lond. Tech. Educ. Gaz.* **5**, 2–17.

Leech, J. (1955). *Proc. Math. Soc. Lond.* **32**, 169.

Leifer, I., G. L. Rogers and N. W. F. Stephens (1969). *Opt. Acta* **16**, 535–553.

Marton, L., (1952). *Phys. Rev.* **85**, 1057.

Marton, L. (1953). *Phys. Rev.* **90**, 490.

Pettigrew, R. M., (1974). *Proceedings of the NELEX 74 Metrology Conference*, NEL, East Kilbride, Glasgow, Paper 20.

Rogers, G. L. (1970). *Handbook of Gas Laser Experiments*, Iliffe and Sons, London, p. 58.

Rogers, G. L. (1974). *Proceedings of the Electro-Optics International Conference,* Brighton, 68–72

Rogers, G. L. and J. C. Davies (1977). *Opt. Commun.* In press.

Stephens, N. W. F. (1971) "Character recognition systems using noncoherent Fourier transformation." Ph.D. Thesis, University of Aston, Birmingham, England.

West, P., (1971). *Metron* 3, 186–192.

Appendix I

Transmission of Information Down an Optical System: Matrix Methods and the Luminance Function

A.1.1. THE LUMINANCE FUNCTION

We can represent the properties of a source by defining a luminance function. Take an area of the source of size $\delta x \cdot \delta y$ centered on x, y in the source plane and consider the luminous flux emitted into a cone of angular size $\delta l \cdot \delta m$ centered on a ray with direction cosines l and m (assumed small). Then the flux is proportional to the size of $\delta x \cdot \delta y$ and of the angular extent $\delta l \cdot \delta m$ and also to some property of the source which is in general a function of x, y, l, m.

Calling the element of flux in this elementary defined region δF we have

$$\delta F = L(x, y, l, m)\, \delta x\, \delta y\, \delta l\, \delta m$$

where $L(x, y, l, m)$ is the luminance function (Figure A.1.1).

Strictly speaking $L(x, y, l, m)$ is also a function of wavelength, but this will not be important in the cases we study.

The ideal source we use in optical data processing has an $L(x, y, l, m)$ that is independent of x and y over a defined region (the source area) and a very slowly varying dependence on l and m. When we place the first input transparency in intimate contact with the source plane, this imposes a function $T_1(x, y)$ on the luminance function, but the slow variation with l and m remains.

130

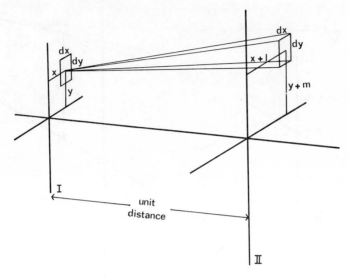

Figure A.1.1 Definition of the luminance function. An area of luminous source in plane I size $\delta x \cdot \delta y$ centered on (x, y) emits a luminous flux into a cone of solid angle $\delta l \cdot \delta m$, with mean direction cosines l and m, and passes through the plane II at a unit distance from plane I. The cone is thus centered on $(x + l, y + m)$ in plane II.

A.1.2. TRANSMISSION OF THE LUMINANCE FUNCTION DOWN THE SYSTEM

We can calculate the luminance function passing from the plane $z = 0$ to the plane $z = z$ by matrix methods. In order to define the physics of the problem, consider the flux passing in the skew prism whose base in the plane $z = 0$ is an element of area $\delta x \cdot \delta y$ centered on the point x, y and whose upper surface is an element in the plane $z = z$ of area $\delta x \cdot \delta y$ centered on the point $(x + lz, y + mz)$ (Figure A.1.2). The average direction of the mean line of this skew prism has direction cosines l and m, and we may take the angular extent of the prism to be $\delta l, \delta m$. The flux δF_0 entering the prism is the same as the flux δF_z leaving the prism, and moreover we have

$$\delta F_0 = L_0(x, y, l, m)\, dx\, dy\, dl\, dm$$
$$\delta F_z = L_z(x + lz, y + mz, l, m)\, dx\, dy\, dl\, dm.$$

so that $L(x, y, lm)$ transposes to $L(x + lx, y + mz, l, m)$ on passage from $z = 0$ to $z = z$.

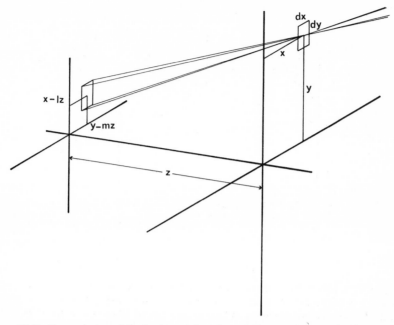

Figure A.1.2 Transmission of the luminance function. The luminance function for an area $dx \times dy$ centered on (x, y) in the second plane $(z = z)$ and emitting along mean direction cosines l and m has come from an area in the first plane $(z = 0)$ centered on $x - lz, y - mz$.

We may express this transposition in matrix form

$$
\begin{vmatrix} x' \\ y' \\ l' \\ m' \end{vmatrix} = \begin{bmatrix} 1 & 0 & +z & 0 \\ 0 & 1 & 0 & +z \\ 0 & 0 & 1 & 0 \\ 0 & 0 & 0 & 1 \end{bmatrix} \times \begin{vmatrix} x \\ y \\ l \\ m \end{vmatrix}
$$

where we put the matrix in square brackets and the column vector on which it operates in straight lines. This 4×4 matrix we call the translation matrix.

A.1.3. THE THIN LENS MATRIX: OPTICAL FOCUSING

When a ray or small pencil of luminous flux strikes a thin lens, its x, y coordinates are unchanged, but its direction cosines are altered by an amount proportional to x or y, respectively. The constant of proportionality, k, is called the *power* of the lens and is the reciprocal of its focal length. In the case of a converging or positive lens, the direction cosines are *reduced* in the positive x, y quadrant, so we have the 4×4 lens matrix in a matrix equation

$$
\begin{vmatrix} x' \\ y' \\ l' \\ m' \end{vmatrix} = \begin{bmatrix} 1 & 0 & 0 & 0 \\ 0 & 1 & 0 & 0 \\ -k & 0 & 1 & 0 \\ 0 & -k & 0 & 1 \end{bmatrix} \times \begin{vmatrix} x \\ y \\ l \\ m \end{vmatrix}
$$

We can now combine a translation matrix from the plane $z = -u$ to $z = 0$ with a lens matrix in the plane $z = 0$ and a further translation matrix to the plane $z = +v$. Without making any particular assumptions about u and v, we obtain by matrix multiplication an operation matrix

$$
\begin{bmatrix} 1 - vk & 0 & v(uk + 1) - u & 0 \\ 0 & 1 - vk & 0 & v(uk + 1) - u \\ -k & 0 & uk + 1 & 0 \\ 0 & -k & 0 & uk + 1 \end{bmatrix}
$$

This general matrix obviously shows a great confusion between x, y, l, m in the input and output planes.

We see, however, that if

$$
v(uk + 1) - u = 0
$$

which is the same as

$$
\frac{1}{v} - \frac{1}{u} = k = \frac{1}{f}
$$

the general matrix reduces to an "in focus" matrix

$$
\begin{bmatrix} \dfrac{v}{u} & 0 & 0 & 0 \\ 0 & \dfrac{v}{u} & 0 & 0 \\ -k & 0 & \dfrac{u}{v} & 0 \\ 0 & -k & 0 & \dfrac{u}{v} \end{bmatrix}
$$

and there is now a one-one relationship between points (x, y) in the input plane and points $(vx/u, vy/u)$ in the output plane: a magnification of v/u.

The rather peculiar factor $-k$ loading the l, m relationship may be overcome by placing a thin lens *in the image plane*. This is called a field lens. Since it is a thin lens it does not affect the x, y coordinates of a point in the image, but only the l, m values. The power of this lens, p, must be such that

$$p = -\frac{u}{v} \cdot k$$

when the "in focus" matrix of a system of an imaging lens and a field lens reduces to the highly symmetrical form

$$\begin{bmatrix} \dfrac{v}{u} & 0 & 0 & 0 \\ 0 & \dfrac{v}{u} & 0 & 0 \\ 0 & 0 & \dfrac{u}{v} & 0 \\ 0 & 0 & 0 & \dfrac{u}{v} \end{bmatrix}$$

We therefore see that the complete luminance function of a source $L_0(x, y, l, m)$ can be reproduced by a suitable optical system either at ± 1 magnification ($v/u = \pm 1$) or under the conditions that the transverse magnification of the x, y coordinates is the inverse of the angular magnification in the l, m domain.

A.1.4. ORTHOGONALITY IN AN OPTICAL SYSTEM

We are now in a position to state the principle of orthogonality in matrix form. Since orthogonal planes *cannot* be conjugate, we must return to the general system matrix

$$\begin{bmatrix} 1 - vk & 0 & v(uk + 1) - u & 0 \\ 0 & 1 - vk & 0 & v(uk + 1) - u \\ -k & 0 & uk + 1 & 0 \\ 0 & -k & 0 & uk + 1 \end{bmatrix}$$

If we now take the input plane in the front focal plane of the lens, and the output plane in the back focal plane, we get

$$u = -f = -\frac{1}{k}$$

$$v = +f = +\frac{1}{k}$$

we find, on substitution in the above, the matrix reduces to:

$$\begin{bmatrix} 0 & 0 & -u & 0 \\ 0 & 0 & 0 & -u \\ -k & 0 & 0 & 0 \\ 0 & -k & 0 & 0 \end{bmatrix}$$

This expresses in matrix form the essential feature of orthogonality, namely that the x, y coordinates in the first plane become transformed into the l, m coordinates of the second plane. It is moreover seen from the equation $u = -1/k$ that the constants of the transformations are reciprocally related (Figure A.1.3).

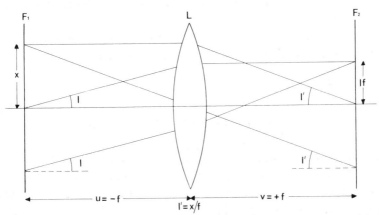

Figure A.1.3 The concept of orthogonality. The front focal plane of a lens and its back focal plane are orthogonal; lateral dimensions in the former are transformed to angular dimensions in the latter, and vice versa.

The orthogonality matrix, taken in conjunction with the "in focus" matrix, shows that planes that are orthogonal in one part of the system, will remain orthogonal if separately imaged onto another part of the system.

A.1.5. THE SPECIAL CASE OF A SEPARABLE LUMINANCE FUNCTION

Although, in general, the luminance function L is a function of x, y, l, m with all the independent variables affecting the output independently, there exists a particular and important class of luminance functions that are separable. In this case, we may write

$$L(x, y, l, m) = T_1(x, y) \cdot T_2(l, m)$$

Thus at any arbitrary point (x_1, y_1) the relative polar diagram $T_2(l, m)$ is the same as at any other arbitrary point (x_2, y_2). Similarly, if viewed in an arbitrary direction (l_1, m_1) the spatial pattern $T_1(x, y)$ will possess the same relative intensities as when viewed in another arbitrary direction (l_2, m_2).

It follows at once from the orthogonality matrix that if L is separable in one orthogonal plane it is separable in the other. The "in focus" matrix leads to a similar conclusion, though in this case $T_2(l, m)$ becomes, to some extent, dependent as to its zero of measurement on x and y, so that a field lens must be used to keep the luminance function strictly separable.

In situations intermediate to these the general translation matrix shows that the luminance function is no longer separable.

A.1.6. IMPORTANCE OF A SEPARABLE LUMINANCE FUNCTION IN NONCOHERENT OPTICAL DATA PROCESSING

A system with a separable luminance function in selected planes is important in optical data processing. In many systems the initial step is to set up a separable luminance function, the two halves of which constitute two sets of input data.

By far the simplest way to construct such a system is to go back to the arrangement described in the section on the orthogonality matrix. We use the usual diffuse extended noncoherent source and place one transparency $T_1(x, y)$ in the front focal plane of a lens and the second transparency $T_2(x, y)$ in the back focal plane. The orthogonality matrix then converts the input $T_1(x, y)$ into a function of l and m independent of x and y in the back focal plane, which is superimposed on $T_2(x, y)$ to give the required luminance function.

We have to bear in mind that orthogonality is defined in terms of the intensity or irradiance pattern, that is, the pattern of luminous intensity resulting when a diffusing screen is placed in a given plane. Such a screen effectively integrates at any point on its surface over all angles of incidence. In this way the intensities in two orthogonal planes may be independent, as the diffuse screen destroys the angular variation pattern which is the only way in which the other plane is represented.

To work out what happens in some general plane, not orthogonal to either of the initial patterns, we must therefore imagine a diffuse screen placed there and integrate over all angles of incidence to calculate the intensity. To achieve this let us draw a diagram (Figure A.1.4) of the system with the separable luminance function and provide ourselves with a separate auxiliary lens to form an image of a virtual plane in the original system onto a diffusing screen. We can then work out the required intensity pattern.

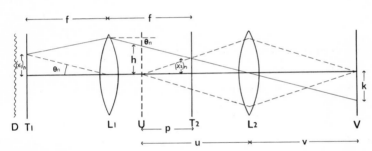

Figure A.1.4 The two-lens correlator. Input transparencies T_1 and T_2 are placed in the front and back focal planes, respectively, of a lens L_1, so as to be orthogonal. They are illuminated from the left by a diffuse source D. A second lens L_2 picks up a plane U in between T_1 and T_2 and images it onto an output plane V. A ray going through L_2 at an angle θ_n to the axis cuts the plane U at a height h and images it on V at a height k. It is found this ray originates at the point $(x_1)_n$ in T_1 and passes through the point $(x_2)_n$ in T_2 thus multiplying the transmissions at these points. When all the rays arriving at k are taken into account we find we have a point in the scaled convolution of T_1 and T_2.

In Figure A.1.4 we have first the usual diffuse extended source illuminating the transparency $T_1(x, y)$ in the front focal plane of the first lens. The second pattern $T_2(x, y)$ in the back focal plane of the same lens completes the input system with the separable luminance function.

The auxiliary lens views a virtual plane a distance p in front of $T_2(x, y)$ and a distance u in front of the lens. It forms a real image of this virtual plane a distance v away on a diffusing screen.

Let us suppose that a ray, traveling in the region between the lenses, makes an angle θ_n with the system axis and is focused by the second lens onto a point a distance k below the axis in the output plane V. It comes from a point a height h above the axis in the virtual plane U conjugate with the output plane. It also follows from the orthogonality matrix that the ray originates from a point $(x_1)_n$ in the plane of $T_1(x, y)$ where

$$\theta_n = \frac{(x_1)_n}{f}$$

It is clear from the diagram that this ray will pass through a point $(x_2)_n$ in the plane of the second pattern $T_2(x, y)$ where

$$\theta_n = \frac{h - (x_2)_n}{p}$$

We therefore have

$$(x_2)_n = h - p \cdot \frac{(x_1)_n}{f}$$

The contribution of this ray to the intensity at the point k depends on the values of the transparency functions T_1 and T_2 at the points $(x_1)_n$ and $(x_2)_n$, respectively. We thus have

$$\delta I(k) = T_1(x_1)_n \cdot T_2(x_2)_n$$

in one dimension. Thus

$$I(k) = \int_{-\infty}^{+\infty} T_1(x_1) \cdot T_2\left(h - p \cdot \frac{x_1}{f}\right) dx_1$$

we can relate $I(k)$ in the output plane V with $I(h)$ in the virtual plane U by use of the lens formula. Since, also, dx_1 is integrated within infinite limits we can change the scale of the x_1 pattern to give

$$I(h) = \int_{-\infty}^{+\infty} T_1\left(\frac{x_1}{p}\right) \times T_2\left(h - \frac{x_1}{f}\right) dx_1$$

Put another way

$$I(h) = T_1\left(\frac{x_1}{p}\right) \circledast T_2\left(\frac{x_2}{f}\right)$$

so that $I(h)$ is the scaled convolution of T_1 and T_2.

Since the focal length f of the first lens and the distance p of the virtual plane from $T_2(x, y)$ are both at our disposal, we can derive from a system with a separable luminance function an intensity pattern that is the convolution of the two separable parts of the luminance function scaled in any proportions. This is an alternative derivation of the result of Dorrestein (1950).

It will be noted that if $p = f$ we get the convolution of T_1 with T_2 on the same scale; that is, the device produces convolutions in the normal sense. This condition means that the auxiliary lens must be focused onto the center of the transform lens. Correlations can be obtained by inverting one of the inputs.

The simple correlator described in Chapter 2 can be reached by a limiting process from the more rigorous convolver of this appendix. The single lens in the simple correlator is equivalent to the auxiliary lens of the rigorous convolver. In this case u_1, and with it p_1 is allowed to tend to infinity, $T_2(x, y)$ remaining in the vicinity of the (auxiliary) lens. At the same time the transform lens also tends to infinity and its focal length becomes infinitely long. The input pattern $T_1(x, y)$ moves off to infinity twice as fast and reappears at minus infinity as images are accustomed to doing. It ends up in the vicinity of $T_2(x, y)$ though not in general in contact with it.

It must be remembered that the simple correlator has a complicated luminance function that is not strictly separable. It only becomes separable when T_1 and T_2 are a long way apart compared with their lateral extent. This can be achieved by suitable control of the limiting process.

It will also be noted that the limiting process implies that $T_1(x, y)$ becomes inverted as it goes through infinity. The rigorous convolution device thus becomes a simple correlator.

REFERENCE

Dorrestein, R. (1950). *Philips Res. Rep.* **5**, 116.

Appendix II

The Number of Independent Channels in an Optical Pathway

In calculations on redundancy, use is frequently made of the idea of the maximum number of channels of communication through the system, and the redundancy is the ratio of this number to the information actually being carried.

We must therefore enquire into the way of calculating this maximum number of channels.

A.2.1. A CHANNEL

In order to define a channel we can imagine an imaging system with a small element of area on the input plane which represents the resolution limit of the system and the corresponding area on the output plane. A photo-emitting diode could be placed on the input area, and a photodetector on the output area, so that a time-varying intensity signal could be passed along the channel. In principle we could also convey a signal by varying the wavelength of the source. We could also alter the state of polarization of the light emitted by the source. But we cannot laterally or angularly subdivide the channel without going beyond the resolution limit and causing confusion between the signals in the two halves. Given that we can always use time variations in intensity, wavelength, and polarization on any one channel, we define the channel in terms of the smallest region which can be isolated without confusion or cross talk.

In a system working under the laws of geometrical optics, the number of channels is infinite; strictly speaking it is quadruply infinite since we have four independent variables in the luminance function. In practice the resolving power of the system is limited by the mean wavelength employed. This gives a theoretical maximum, which can be quite easily calculated. There may, in practice, be further considerations, such as aberrations in the system, that will reduce the number of channels which can be used without cross talk or by using some very complex system for eliminating cross modulation; for example, by correlation with a point spread function.

A.2.2. THE ETENDU OF A SYSTEM

An important physical measure of the light-handling capacity of a system is its Etendu. This idea is widely used in spectroscopy where it gives a useful measure of the speed of the spectrograph. We shall find that the information-handling capacity of the system is proportional to its light-handling capacity.

Let us suppose that the system has an input field of area A_1, which we shall take to be a rectangle of size $B \times C$ units of length (Figure A.2.1). It will also have an entrance pupil of area A_2 and size $G \times H$ units: in the case of a spectrograph this is normally the entrance slit. The advantage of the Girard grille and the Fourier spectroscope is, of course, that the entrance pupil can be large. Let us suppose that the field and entrance pupil are both substantially perpendicular to a line of sight and

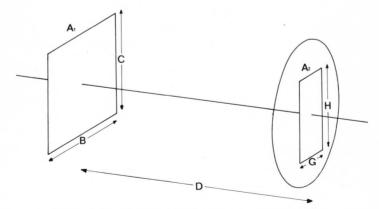

Figure A.2.1 Etendu and information-carrying capacity.

that they are situated a distance D apart along this line. Assume $D \gg B$, C, G, H.

We can now *define* the Etendu of the system by any of three equivalent definitions

   1. E = Field area × angular size of entrance pupil at center of field.

   2. E = Entrance pupil area × angular size of the field at center of entrance pupil.

   3. $= \dfrac{A_1 A_2}{D^2}.$

It will be seen that Etendu has the dimension of an area.

A.2.3. CALCULATION OF THE NUMBER OF INDEPENDENT CHANNELS

If we seek to determine the size of a patch in the field at the limit of resolution of the system, we note that the finite size of the entrance pupil gives rise to limits to the angular resolving power of the system, which in the case of a rectangular entrance pupil are different in the two directions. Calling these resolutions $\delta\theta$ and $\delta\phi$, respectively, we have

$$\delta\theta = \frac{\lambda}{G} \qquad \delta\phi = \frac{\lambda}{H}$$

If we project this solid angular cone onto the field at a distance D we get an area on the field plane of

$$D^2\, \delta\theta\, \delta\phi = \frac{D^2\lambda^2}{GH} = \frac{D^2\lambda^2}{A_2}$$

This represents the size of a channel at the input plane.

The number of independent channels through the system is thus the ratio of A_1 to this elementary area, or

$$N = \frac{A_1}{D^2\lambda^2/A_2} = \frac{A_1 A_2}{D^2\lambda^2} = \frac{E}{\lambda^2}$$

The number of independent channels through an optical system working at the wavelength limit of resolution is therefore

$$N = (\text{Etendu})/\lambda^2$$

a dimensionless quantity.

Appendix III

The Production of
a Uniform Source

Chapter 2 emphasizes the importance of a uniform source, and this is reinforced in Chapter 6, where methods are described for improving the low contrast of the output which depend critically on the use of a uniform source in the first place. Algebraic analysis can be used up to a point with simplifying assumptions, but when realistic assumptions come to be made about possible small inequalities in the individual lamps in a source, computer tabulated results are an invaluable guide.

A.3.1. THE ILLUMINATION FROM A SINGLE SOURCE

In the first place let us consider the illumination falling into a horizontal plane from a uniform source of strength P a vertical height h above it. The illumination diagram is circularly symmetrical so that the illumination can be sufficiently defined in terms of the radial distance r, from the foot of the perpendicular from the source onto the plane (Figure A.3.1).

The illumination at any point is inversely proportional to the square of its distance from the source and directly proportional to the cosine of the angle θ between the ray and the normal to the plane at the point in question. We can, therefore, write

$$I = \frac{P \cos \theta}{r^2 + h^2} = \frac{P}{r^2 + h^2} \cdot \frac{h}{\sqrt{r^2 + h^2}} = \frac{Ph}{(r^2 + h^2)^{3/2}}$$

In our application we are only concerned with the relative illumination

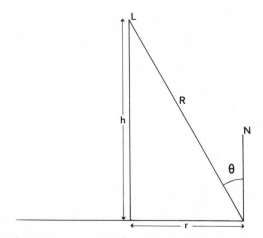

Figure A.3.1 Illumination from a single lamp L at a distance r from the foot of the perpendicular height h is $P \cos \theta / R^2$ where θ is the angle of the ray from the surface normal and R is the hypotenuse distance from the lamp to the point illuminated. P is the power of the lamp.

at different points in the plane, and this can be expressed in terms of the parameter r/h. Thus

$$I = \frac{Ph}{\left(\dfrac{r^2}{h^2}+1\right)^{3/2} \cdot h^{3/2}} = \frac{p}{h^{1/2}\left(\dfrac{r^2}{h^2}+1\right)^{3/2}}$$

In relative measurements we can, therefore, use the function

$$\frac{1}{\left(\dfrac{r^2}{h^2}+1\right)^{3/2}}$$

as a measurement of the illumination.

On this basis we arrange that the illumination at the foot of the perpendicular is normalized to 1, and we can find the place where the illumination has fallen to some specified value, say, 0.9, by solving an equation of the type

$$\frac{1}{\left(\dfrac{r^2}{h^2}+1\right)^{3/2}} = 0.9$$

An approximate solution of this is $r = 0.27\,h$. Hence, within a circle of diameter half the height of the source, the illumination is uniform to 10%. If the plane is a translucent Lambertian diffuser, the light emerging from the far side is also uniform to 10%. This is the basis of the illuminating boxes widely used in our laboratory.

A.3.2. ILLUMINATION FROM FOUR EQUAL SOURCES PLACED AT THE CORNERS OF A SQUARE

The next approximation to producing a uniform field of illumination is to place four equal sources at the corners of a square. It simplifies the algebra if we make the side of this square $2a$, the height of the sources above this plane being h. Figure A.3.2 illustrates the arrangement and defines the coordinates.

We now have to add four illumination terms of the type given above, substituting for four different values of r from the Cartesian coordinates in the square. Taking our origin at the center of the square, and (x, y) as

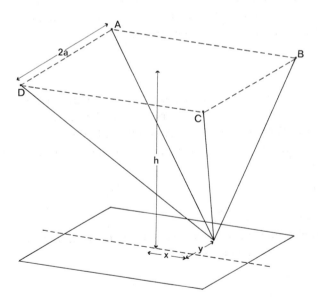

Figure A.3.2 Illumination by four lamps A, B, C, D, at the corners of a square of side $2a$. The plane of the lamps are at a height h from the plane of illumination. x, y are the coordinates of the point of illumination referred to the point of symmetry. The illumination is given by the formula in the text.

the coordinates of a particular point in the field we get

$$I(x, y) = Ph \left\{ \frac{1}{[h^2 + (x + a)^2 + (y + a)^2]^{3/2}} + \frac{1}{[h^2 + (x - a)^2 + (y + a)^2]^{3/2}} \right.$$

$$\left. + \frac{1}{[h^2 + (x + a)^2 + (y - a)^2]^{3/2}} + \frac{1}{[h^2 + (x - a)^2 + (y - a)^2]^{3/2}} \right\}$$

It is readily shown that with this function $dI/dr = 0$ at the center $(x = 0, y = 0)$; that is, the illumination at the center is either a maximum, a minimum, or a point of inflection. In order to get as large a central area of uniform illumination as possible we have to find the condition for a point of inflection $d^2I/dr^2 = 0$.

The process of differentiating $I(x, y)$ twice is tedious rather than intrinsically difficult, and the result is that a point of inflection occurs when

$$h^2 = 3a^2$$

This point of inflection gives a very uniform area of illumination around the center of the square below the lamps, but the illumination falls off at the edges of the square. To compensate for this we move into the region where

$$h^2 < 3a^2$$

It is readily shown that we require $h > 2a^2$, since this gives noticeably brighter illumination at the corners than at the center.

To investigate the behavior between these limits, a computer was used to calculate the field at intervals $0.1a$ in x and y for steps of 0.1 in the equation

$$h^2 = (2 + n \times 0.1)a^2$$

with n running from 0 to 10.

It is found empirically that the most uniform illumination within the square of side $2a$ occurs when

$$h^2 = 2.5a^2$$

To illustrate this we have only to plot the field in one quadrant, since the symmetry of the system repeats this field by reflection in the other quadrants. This is plotted in Figure A.3.3 where we have taken the

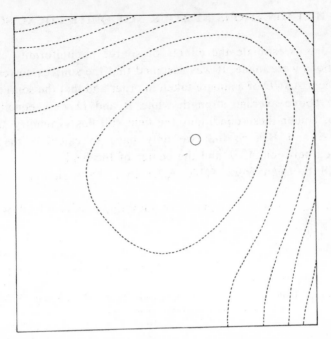

Figure A.3.3 Isophotes in first quadrant of a surface illuminated by a square of lamps, side $2a$, at a height h where $h^2 = 2.5a^2$. The point O represents an intensity of 100% and successive isophotes represent intensities of 99%, 98%, ..., 95%. The pattern over the whole area of illumination is obtained by reflection in the symmetry axes lying along left-hand edge and bottom of the diagram.

brightest point part way along the diagonal between center and one lamp as 100%. The contours drawn represent regions 1%, 2%, and so forth, down on this 100% illumination. It is readily seen that the whole square is uniformly illuminated to 6% and that a large part of it is uniformly illuminated to 2%.

In many practical situations it is possible to make the side of the square $2a$, defining the position of the lamps, 60–70% larger than the square one wishes to illuminate. Under these conditions very favorable results can be obtained. In the point of inflection case, the illumination in a square of side $1.2a$ properly centered lies within 1% all over and the variation falls to 0.5% within a square of side a. Such calculated uniformity can, however, be quite illusory since it assumes an equality of source strength unlikely to be achieved in practice.

A.3.3. ILLUMINATIONS BY FOUR NOT QUITE EQUAL SOURCES

In order to estimate the effects of source nonuniformity simplified calculations were made. It was assumed that the sources correspond to the corners $ABCD$ of a square taken in order and that the sources A and C were above average strength while B and D were equally below average. Under these conditions the field still has symmetry about the lines AC and BD, so that we only have to calculate the triangle contained between A, B, and the center of the field.

It will be seen from Table A.3.1 that the variation in the field

TABLE A.3.1. EFFECT OF SOURCE POWER VARIATIONS ON UNIFORMITY OF THE FIELD

Case $h^2 = 3a^2$

Percentage Departure of Lamps from Mean	Percentage Variation in Field	
	Square Side 1.2a	Square Side 1.0a
2%	1.29%	0.70%
5%	2.07%	1.35%
10%	3.62%	2.65%

uniformity is less than the variation in lamp power. Thus a ±5% variation in lamp power produces an overall variation of 2% on the 1.2a field and of 1.35% on the 1.0a field. With a little care in choice of lamps, using a photometer, lamps can be matched to 5% and they can be placed around the square to produce the best compensation; for example, A and C above average and B and D below average. Under these circumstances field uniformity of the order of 2% can be obtained.

A.3.4. MORE COMPLEX ILLUMINATING SYSTEMS

There is no limit to the ingenuity that can be expended in devising more complex illuminating systems, for example, those using line sources of light such as fluorescent tubes. Readers who feel tempted to explore such systems may like to know that empirical rules exist to guide them.

The problem of obtaining a uniformly illuminated surface, using sources of light a fixed distance h above it, is formally similar to the problem of giving a uniform dose of gamma radiation to a superficial tumor by arranging a set of radium needles or radon seeds on a flat surface held close to the tumor. For good and sufficient medical reasons, this subject has been intensively studied, and as a result a set of rules known as Patterson's rules are now widely used in radiology (Patterson et al. 1936, 1938).

The rules are to some extent colored by the very weak sources generally available in the 1930s, which means that a very close approach is desirable to avoid inverse square law loss. The procedure of choice is, therefore, to use a fairly large number of small sources arranged in a series of rings, sometimes containing a center. Rules for determining the number of rings and their sizes have been given by Patterson. Interested readers are referred to the original papers for details. Very often a Patterson arrangement is a useful starting point for calculations.

A.3.5. POSSIBLE COMPENSATION FOR VIGNETTING EFFECTS

One of the other sources of an uneven output in an optical processor is vignetting; that is, tendency for oblique pencils to get partially cut off by the apertures and stops in the system. This leads to an output that falls off toward the edge of the field. In principle it might be possible to secure partial compensation for this effect by deliberately making the edge of the source brighter than the center. This is done by reducing h relative to a, to give more light in the corners.

This idea has not been explored in practice, and it would require some detailed calculations to arrive at a worthwhile arrangement. It is far safer to make the optical apertures larger than the theoretical minimum. For one thing, having a source which is brighter at the periphery is equivalent to biassing the input function at the edge of the field. This would require detailed justification. In a case of bad vignetting the distortion of the input function might be tolerable for the sake of a more uniform output field allowing higher contrast amplification.

A.3.6. USE OF AN UNSHARP MASK

In the case where the output of an optical processor is recorded on a photographic plate, it is sometimes possible to compensate partially for nonuniformities in the background by the use of an unsharp mask.

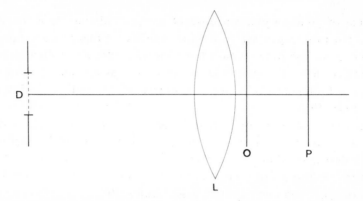

Figure A.3.4   Making an unsharp mask. A relatively small diffuse source *D* is placed in the focal plane of the lens *L*. The object to be masked (generally a photographic plate or transparency of the output to be corrected) is at *O* and a blurred negative is recorded at *P*. After developing *P* to a low contrast, *O* and *P* are bound together in contact and projection printed

If a rectangular diffuse white source is placed in the focal plane of a large lens (Figure A.3.4.) whose size is larger than the output photograph, an unsharp mask can be made by taking a noncontact print from the output. The fact that the source is in the focal plane of the collimating lens means there is no projective magnification between the output plate and the noncontact print (Alqazzaz 1976).

The noncontact print or mask, which should be made on a transparent base, is ideally developed to a gamma of 1, though lower gammas are often used. After processing it may be brought into register with the output, and the sandwich is projection-printed in an enlarger.

Because the fine structure is lost in the noncontact print the mask will not obscure the fine detail in the output, but it will alter the local DC bias in a sense beneficial to obtaining a print of uniform total level.

As always with systems that involve subtraction, the noise is added and this must always be taken into account.

It is also possible to get local contrast reversal if the mask is overdeveloped. Many operators, therefore, prefer to hold the contrast of the mask down. Gammas as low as 0.3–0.45 have been used.

The process is not entirely satisfactory unless the degree of nonuniformity is moderate. If too large a range of densities is required in the mask, the overall density of the sandwich is too high for satisfactory projection printing.

ACKNOWLEDGMENTS

I am much indebted to Mr. J. C. Davies for writing the computer programs needed for this study and for running them for me.

REFERENCES

Alqazzaz, L. (1976). Ph.D. Thesis. University of Aston, Birmingham, England.

Patterson, R., H. M. Parker, and F. W. Spiers (1936). *Br. J. Radiol.* **9**, 487–508.

Patterson, R. and H. M. Parker (1938) *Br. J. Radiol.* **11**, 252–266.

Appendix IV

Matrix Methods for Polarized Light

A.4.1. PLANE POLARIZED LIGHT

A beam of plane polarized light is one in which the electrostatic vector remains in a fixed direction, perpendicular to the direction of propagation. It is, therefore, an example of a transverse wave. In an isotropic medium, whose properties are independent of direction, it obeys Maxwells equations one of which may be written in this form

$$\mathbf{D} = \epsilon \cdot \mathbf{E}$$

where ϵ is a scalar constant called the permitivity. It follows that, in an isotropic medium, the vectors $\mathbf{D}$ and $\mathbf{E}$ lie in the same direction, and the solution to Maxwells equations is a progressive wave moving with a constant velocity.

Most polarization effects arise when such a beam strikes an anisotropic medium. In this case, the above equation must be written

$$\mathbf{D} = [\epsilon] \cdot \mathbf{E}$$

where $[\epsilon]$ is no longer a scalar, but a tensor (sometimes called a linear vector operator). In general one will find directions such that $[\epsilon]$ reduces to a scalar. That is, if $\mathbf{E}$ happens to be along one of the principal directions, $\mathbf{D}$ is parallel to it. Again, in general, there will be three different constants of proportionality, ϵ_1, ϵ_2, and ϵ_3, one for each principal direction.

If **E** lies in some direction, not a principal one, the effect of the operator $[\epsilon]$ on **E** is to resolve it into three components along the principal directions, multiply each component by the appropriate factor ϵ_1, ϵ_2, or ϵ_3, and then recombine them to form **D**. It follows at once that **D** is *not* parallel to **E** and that the solution to Maxwells equations is not a single progressive wave.

In practice, a single progressive wave in an isotropic medium usually falls at some angle onto the surface of an anisotropic medium, and thereafter breaks up into *two* progressive waves polarized at right angles. The directions of vibration are determined by the principal directions of the anisotropic medium and the velocities of propagation are different. Phase differences therefore arise between the two waves.

When these waves fall on the interface with a second anisotropic medium, there exist once again two possible vibration directions related to the principal directions of the second medium. Two progressive waves exist in the second medium. To arrive at their amplitudes, the waves in the first medium have to be resolved and recombined (allowing for phase shifts) in the new directions. The basic mathematics is relatively simple but it can become cumbersome unless shortcuts are taken.

A.4.2. UNIAXIAL MATERIALS

Many of the effects we are interested in can be studied relatively simply because they can be realized in uniaxial materials. These are anisotropic but have the particular property that $\epsilon_1 = \epsilon_2 \neq \epsilon_3$. The direction associated with ϵ_3 is called the optic axial direction, or more simply the optic axis, since any waves traveling in direction 3 must vibrate in the plane of $\epsilon_1\epsilon_2$ and thus they all have the same velocity.

A thin slab of uniaxial material (generally a uniaxial crystal) cut with the optic axis in the plane of the lamina is called a principal section of the crystal. Most of the effects we seek can be obtained by propagating a polarized beam perpendicular to the principal section of a uniaxial crystal, but with its polarization directions, in general, oblique to the optic axis of the crystal.

A.4.3.   A FULLY POLARIZED BEAM

A fully polarized beam of light is one not mixed with unpolarized light. It is generally produced by passing light through a polarizer and then through other elements. It is characterized by the fact that it is always possible to devise a system of elements that will convert it onto a plane polarized beam which can be extinguished with a polarizer or passed. at maximum intensity when the polarizer is swung 90° from extinction. Such a beam can be characterized if we know that complex amplitude components in two directions at right angles. If unpolarized light is added, at least four parameters are required to specify the light, but we shall not need to consider this case.

The fully polarized beam only has three independent parameters, the moduli of the complex amplitudes and the *phase difference* between the two components. In practice, we often carry the absolute phases through our calculations, especially when the device is designed to introduce a calculated phase shift into the wave.

A.4.4.   PLANE POLARIZED LIGHT FALLING ONTO A PRINCIPAL SECTION OF A UNIAXIAL CRYSTAL

Let us suppose we have a principal section of a uniaxial crystal lying in the plane XOY with its optic axis along OX (Figure A.4.1). Suppose now a plane polarized wave strikes the far side with the direction of vibration making an angle θ with OX. The wave breaks up into two components

$$x = a \cos \theta \sin \omega t = a_1 \sin \omega t$$

$$y = a \sin \theta \sin \omega t = a_2 \sin \omega t$$

with $\tan \theta = a_2/a_1$.

Because of the difference of speed in the crystal, the waves emerge with a phase difference from the front surface of the slab. Let this phase difference be ϕ, with the x vibration behind the y vibration. Then we have components

$$x = a_1 \sin \omega t$$

$$y = a_2 \sin (\omega t + \phi)$$

Eliminating "ωt" from these, we find the electrostatic vector traces out

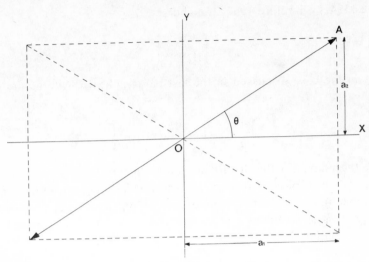

Figure A.4.1 A polarized beam, vibrating along *OA*, falls on a principal section of a uniaxial crystal, optic axis *OX*. The angle $AOX = \theta$. The polarized beam is split into components a_1 and a_2, and when these emerge there is a relative phase difference between them giving, in general, an elliptical disturbance.

an ellipse

$$\frac{y^2}{a_2^2} - 2\frac{xy}{a_1 a_2}\cos\phi + \frac{x^2}{a_1^2} - \sin^2\phi = 0$$

This is an ellipse with its major axis making an angle ψ with *OX* given by

$$\tan 2\psi = \tan 2\theta \cdot \cos\phi$$

Hence if $\theta = 45°$; $\psi = 45°$ but otherwise ψ is a function of ϕ.

We have to discuss whether the vector is rotating clockwise or counterclockwise. Since y is leading on x by what we shall assume is a moderate amount, we get a right-handed elliptically polarized light. In the special case where $\theta = 45°$, $\phi = 90°$, the ellipse becomes a circle.

A.4.5. MATRIX REPRESENTATION OF CRYSTAL OPERATIONS

First of all we note that a *completely* polarized beam of light, such as we shall be using in our applications, can be represented by a column vector giving first the x and then the y component in complex notation

(Jones 1941; Shurcliffe 1962; Longhurst 1973)

$$\left| \begin{array}{c} A_x\, e^{-i\delta_x} \\ A_y\, e^{-i\delta_y} \end{array} \right|$$

Thus in the case discussed in the last paragraph, we have as the input vector

$$\left| \begin{array}{c} a\cos\theta \\ a\sin\theta \end{array} \right| \quad \text{or} \quad \left| \begin{array}{c} a_1 \\ a_2 \end{array} \right|$$

since the phases of the disturbances are equal.

The effect of passing through the crystal slab is to introduce a phase difference between the two components. In the analysis given above we have chosen to introduce a phase advance into the y component by the matrix equation

$$\left| \begin{array}{c} a_1 \\ a_2\, e^{i\phi} \end{array} \right| = \left[\begin{array}{cc} 1 & 0 \\ 0 & e^{i\phi} \end{array} \right] \times \left| \begin{array}{c} a_1 \\ a_2 \end{array} \right|$$

So that we can represent the effect of the crystal slab by the matrix

$$\left[\begin{array}{cc} 1 & 0 \\ 0 & e^{i\phi} \end{array} \right]$$

where we put the matrix in square brackets to distinguish it from the column vectors between straight lines.

We could equally have "split the difference" and written our matrix

$$\left[\begin{array}{cc} e^{-i\phi/2} & 0 \\ 0 & e^{+i\phi/2} \end{array} \right]$$

though if we do this we must be careful with systems producing phase shifts that the phase changes are correctly added through the system.

A.4.6.   THE ROTATION MATRIX

One of the most tedious features of polarized light calculations is that successive elements, for example, crystal slabs cut in principal sections, typically have their optic axes arranged at all sorts of angles around the direction of propagation. In the old system this required resolution of the disturbances freshly for every plate. The equivalent effect can be

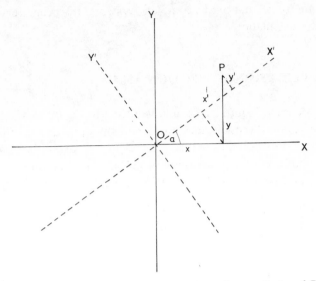

Figure A.4.2 Derivation of the rotation matrix. (x, y) are the coordinates of P in the first system of axes XOY and $(x'y')$ the coordinates in the second system $X'O'Y'$. The rotation of axes through an angle α transforms (x, y) into (x', y') (see text).

produced by matrix methods by inserting a rotation matrix between successive components.

In Figure A.4.2 we have a system of axes XOY representing the output of the nth crystal, with, say, OX being its optic axis. The system of axes $X'OY'$ represents the input to the $(n + 1)$th crystal, with its optic axis OX' making a positive angle α with OX. By taking components along the new axes we obtain a rotation matrix

$$\begin{bmatrix} \cos \alpha & \sin \alpha \\ -\sin \alpha & \cos \alpha \end{bmatrix}$$

This must be inserted in the correct position between the operation matrices of the nth and $(n + 1)$th crystal slabs. As in matrix algebra, the first matrix is placed on the right and each successive matrix, as the light passes through the system, is placed just to the left of the previous matrix. Finally, we can condense the string of matrices into the "system matrix" which gives the effect of the system as a whole on any input column vector, without detailed calculations as to what happens in between

$$\mathbf{M} = M_n \times M_{n-1} \times \cdots \times M_k \times \cdots \times M_2 \times M_1$$

It will be seen that with complex systems this can very greatly simplify the calculations.

A.4.7.   APPLICATION TO SECTION A.4.4

We can redraw Figure A.4.1 in the form of Figure A.4.3, with the input polarization direction horizontal, and the optic axis of the slab at an angle of $-\theta$ to the horizontal.

A horizontally vibrating polarized beam has an x component but no y component and hence may be represented by the column vector

$$\begin{vmatrix} 1 \\ 0 \end{vmatrix}$$

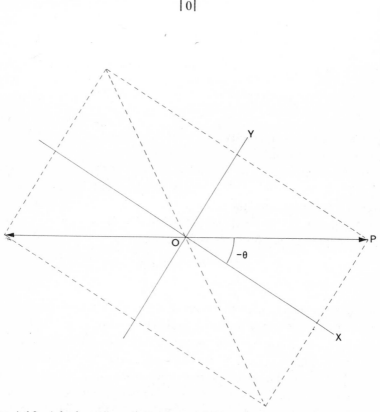

Figure A.4.3   A horizontally polarized beam of light falls on the principal section of a uniaxial crystal with its optic axis (OX) making an angle $-\theta$ with the polarization direction.

where we adopt the convention that the input vector should be normalized to give unit intensity.

Next we have to introduce a rotation matrix for an angle $-\theta$ to give

$$\begin{vmatrix} \cos\theta \\ \sin\theta \end{vmatrix} = \begin{bmatrix} \cos\theta & -\sin\theta \\ \sin\theta & \cos\theta \end{bmatrix} \times \begin{vmatrix} 1 \\ 0 \end{vmatrix}$$

We now apply the phase shift matrix of the crystal slab in the symmetrical form, giving

$$\begin{bmatrix} e^{-i\phi/2} & 0 \\ 0 & e^{+i\phi/2} \end{bmatrix} \times \begin{bmatrix} \cos\theta & -\sin\theta \\ \sin\theta & \cos\theta \end{bmatrix}$$

and finally we can rotate through $+\theta$ to get back to our original axes

$$\begin{bmatrix} \cos\theta & \sin\theta \\ -\sin\theta & \cos\theta \end{bmatrix} \times \begin{bmatrix} e^{-i\phi/2} & 0 \\ 0 & e^{+i\phi/2} \end{bmatrix} \times \begin{bmatrix} \cos\theta & -\sin\theta \\ \sin\theta & \cos\theta \end{bmatrix}$$

A.4.8. PARTICULAR CASES

The general solution of the above matrix equation is not very helpful, but there are particular cases where it is very instructive.

A.4.8.1. The Halfwave Plate

1. If $\phi = \pi$, or half a wavelength the slab is called a *halfwave* plate, and the central matrix reduces to

$$\begin{bmatrix} i & 0 \\ 0 & -i \end{bmatrix}$$

The system matrix now reduces to

$$\begin{bmatrix} -\cos 2\theta & \sin 2\theta \\ \sin 2\theta & \cos 2\theta \end{bmatrix}$$

If we allow this to operate on a plane polarized wave in the x direction we get

$$\begin{vmatrix} -\cos 2\theta \\ +\sin 2\theta \end{vmatrix} = \begin{bmatrix} -\cos 2\theta & \sin 2\theta \\ \sin 2\theta & \cos 2\theta \end{bmatrix} \times \begin{vmatrix} 1 \\ 0 \end{vmatrix}$$

This corresponds to a plane polarized beam at an angle -2θ. Since the optic axis is displaced an angle $-\theta$ from the horizontal axis, this means that the plane of polarization is "rotated" through twice the angle of misalignment of the optic axis. More strictly it should be regarded as reflected in the optic axis. This is the basis of the Jaumann modulator.

A.4.8.2.   Symmetry Between Polarizer and Plate

2. If $\theta = \pi/4$ we get an interesting result, since the ellipse produced now always has its major axis either horizontal or vertical.

The system matrix becomes

$$\frac{1}{\sqrt{2}}\begin{bmatrix} 1 & 1 \\ -1 & 1 \end{bmatrix} \times \begin{bmatrix} e^{-i\phi/2} & 0 \\ 0 & e^{+i\phi/2} \end{bmatrix} \times \frac{1}{\sqrt{2}}\begin{bmatrix} 1 & -1 \\ 1 & 1 \end{bmatrix}$$

which reduces to

$$\begin{bmatrix} \cos \phi/2 & i \sin \phi/2 \\ i \sin \phi/2 & \cos \phi/2 \end{bmatrix}$$

The effect of this on a horizontally polarized beam is

$$\begin{vmatrix} \cos \phi/2 \\ i \sin \phi/2 \end{vmatrix} = \begin{bmatrix} \cos \phi/2 & i \sin \phi/2 \\ i \sin \phi/2 & \cos \phi/2 \end{bmatrix} = \begin{vmatrix} 1 \\ 0 \end{vmatrix}$$

which is an elliptical vibration, whose axis in the x direction is $\cos \phi/2$ and in the y direction is $\sin \phi/2$.

A.4.8.3.   The Quarter Wave Plate

3. If θ is arbitrary and $\phi = \pi/2$ we note that $\phi = \pi/2$ introduces a quarter wave delay and the slab is called a *quarter wave plate*.

The central matrix now becomes

$$\begin{bmatrix} e^{-i\pi/4} & 0 \\ 0 & e^{+i\pi/4} \end{bmatrix} = e^{-i\pi/4}\begin{bmatrix} 1 & 0 \\ 0 & +i \end{bmatrix}$$

so that one vibration is shifted into quadrature relative to the other.

If we consider what happens if this operates on a linearly polarized input at $\theta = \pi/4$ we get (dropping the $e^{-i\pi/4}$)

$$\begin{bmatrix} 1 & 0 \\ 0 & +i \end{bmatrix} \times \frac{1}{\sqrt{2}}\begin{bmatrix} 1 & -1 \\ 1 & 1 \end{bmatrix} \times \begin{vmatrix} 1 \\ 0 \end{vmatrix}$$

$$= \begin{bmatrix} 1 & 0 \\ 0 & +i \end{bmatrix} \times \frac{1}{\sqrt{2}}\begin{vmatrix} 1 \\ 1 \end{vmatrix} = \frac{1}{\sqrt{2}}\begin{vmatrix} 1 \\ i \end{vmatrix}$$

which is a circularly polarized beam.

A.4.9. QUARTER WAVE PLATE FOLLOWING CRYSTAL SECTION

If $\theta = \pi/4$ we get that a crystal slab of phase delay ϕ has a matrix

$$\begin{bmatrix} \cos \phi/2 & i \sin \phi/2 \\ i \sin \phi/2 & \cos \phi/2 \end{bmatrix}$$

if after this we place a quarter wave plate with its optic axis horizontal we get

$$\begin{bmatrix} 1 & 0 \\ 0 & +i \end{bmatrix} \times \begin{bmatrix} \cos \phi/2 & i \sin \phi/2 \\ i \sin \phi/2 & \cos \phi/2 \end{bmatrix}$$

$$= \begin{bmatrix} \cos \phi/2 & i \sin \phi/2 \\ -\sin \phi/2 & i \cos \phi/2 \end{bmatrix}$$

If the input light is once again horizontally polarized we get

$$\begin{vmatrix} \cos \phi/2 \\ -\sin \phi/2 \end{vmatrix} = \begin{bmatrix} \cos \phi/2 & i \sin \phi/2 \\ -\sin \phi/2 & i \cos \phi/2 \end{bmatrix} \times \begin{vmatrix} 1 \\ 0 \end{vmatrix}$$

Thus the output is plane polarized light inclined at $-\phi/2$ to the horizontal.

A.4.10. THE ELECTRO-OPTIC ROTATOR

If now the crystal slab is an electro-optic crystal whose delay is dependent on the applied voltage ($\phi \alpha V$), we see that we now have the basis of an electro-optic rotator. If ϕ is swung from $-\pi$ to $+\pi$ and then jumps back owing to a saw-toothed voltage drive, the angle of the polarized beam emerging from the system rotates from $-\pi/2$ to $+\pi/2$ and appears to go on rotating after fly-back. This is the system of Figure 8.10.

It should also be noted that if the crystal slab is a normal crystal with unknown phase delay ϕ, we can use this system to determine ϕ by measuring the angle between the emergent polarization and the axis of the quarter wave plate (assuming $\theta = \pi/4$ has first been obtained).

It is of interest that if the quarter wave plate is imperfect, for example, if it shifts the phase by 80° instead of 90°, it will still measure ϕ to around 1°. In this way, starting with an imperfect quarter wave plate, we can select a better one and so on.

A.4.11. THE CIRCULAR POLARISCOPE

We have seen in Chapter 8 that a circular polariscope can be used to give a phase shifting device. The circular polariscope starts with a polarizer and a quarter wave plate with its optic axis (say the fast axis) at 45° to the polarizer, as we saw earlier this gives an output.

$$\frac{1}{\sqrt{2}}\begin{vmatrix} 1 \\ i \end{vmatrix}$$

or in our case a right-handed circularly polarized beam.

It is instructive to consider what happens if we operate on this vector with a rotation matrix; that is, if we refer it to axes inclined to the original axes. It is readily shown that we get

$$\frac{1}{\sqrt{2}}\begin{bmatrix} \cos\alpha & \sin\alpha \\ -\sin\alpha & \cos\alpha \end{bmatrix} \times \begin{vmatrix} 1 \\ i \end{vmatrix} = \frac{1}{\sqrt{2}}\begin{vmatrix} \cos\alpha & +i\sin\alpha \\ -\sin\alpha & +i\cos\alpha \end{vmatrix}$$

$$= \frac{1}{\sqrt{2}}\begin{vmatrix} e^{i\alpha} \\ ie^{i\alpha} \end{vmatrix} = \frac{e^{i\alpha}}{\sqrt{2}}\begin{vmatrix} 1 \\ i \end{vmatrix}$$

This is still a circularly polarized beam but we have phase shifted it by an angle α.

A.4.12. INTRODUCTION OF A HALFWAVE PLATE: THE SINGLE SIDEBAND MODULATOR

We have already seen that the introduction of a halfwave plate will shift the plane of polarization of a plane polarized beam. Its effect on a circularly polarized beam is twofold. It turns a right-handed beam, into a left-handed beam, and it introduces a phase shift.

We have already seen the matrix of a halfwave plate is

$$\begin{bmatrix} i & 0 \\ 0 & -i \end{bmatrix}$$

so that if this operates on R. H. polarized light we get

$$\begin{bmatrix} i & 0 \\ 0 & -i \end{bmatrix} \times \frac{1}{\sqrt{2}}\begin{vmatrix} 1 \\ i \end{vmatrix} = \frac{1}{\sqrt{2}}\begin{vmatrix} i \\ 1 \end{vmatrix}$$

which is of course left-handed circularly polarized light as the relative phase shift of the two components is reversed.

It follows that if a halfwave plate is introduced into a circular polariscope originally set for extinction, as in Figure 8.8, the effect is to allow light to pass.

We have also seen that if the halfwave plate has its axis lying on angle θ below the horizontal its system matrix is

$$\begin{bmatrix} -\cos 2\theta & \sin 2\theta \\ \sin 2\theta & \cos 2\theta \end{bmatrix}$$

and if this operates on R. H. circularly polarized light we get

$$\begin{bmatrix} -\cos 2\theta & \sin 2\theta \\ \sin 2\theta & \cos 2\theta \end{bmatrix} \times \frac{1}{\sqrt{2}} \begin{vmatrix} 1 \\ i \end{vmatrix} = \frac{1}{\sqrt{2}} \begin{vmatrix} -\cos 2\theta & +i\sin 2\theta \\ \sin 2\theta & +i\cos 2\theta \end{vmatrix}$$

$$= \frac{1}{\sqrt{2}} \begin{vmatrix} -e^{-2i\theta} \\ ie^{-2i\theta} \end{vmatrix} = \frac{e^{-2i\theta}}{\sqrt{2}} \begin{vmatrix} -1 \\ i \end{vmatrix}$$

which is L. H. Circular polarized light, phase shifted by 2θ. If θ varies steadily with time, owing to the rotation of the halfwave plate, the output phase also varies steadily. This is equivalent to a small shift of input frequency.

It is relatively simple, if tedious, to set up the matrix equation in reverse to show that if the light travels through the system backward, the phase shift is also reversed. If such a system, that is a single sideband modulator, is inserted in a triangular interferometer, it will impose opposite phase shifts on the beams circulating in opposite directions around the interferometer.

REFERENCES

Longhurst, R. S. (1973). *Geometrical and Physical Optics*, 3rd ed., Longman, London, p. 562–565.

Jones, R. C. (1941). *J. Opt. Soc. Amer.* **31**, 488–503.

Shurcliffe, W. A. (1962). *Polarized Light*, Oxford University Press, Oxford.

Appendix V

A Note on
Partial Coherence

Although in classical optics it is customary to regard a situation as either coherent or noncoherent, the idea was introduced in the 1930s that an intermediate region exists where the situation is partially coherent. The pioneer papers were by Van Cittert (1934, 1939) and Zernike (1937a, b, 1938, 1948) and after the war a large number of papers were published by Wolf (1954, 1955), Hopkins (1951, 1953), and others (Mandel and Wolf 1965).

A.5.1. THE YOUNG DOUBLE SLIT AS A TEST OF COHERENCE

The basic idea is this. If a Young double slit is illuminated by a very fine monochromatic or quasi-monochromatic source slit some distance away, interference fringes of high contrast result. It is important to realize that *in the plane of the source*, the atomic events are uncoordinated and the source is therefore noncoherent. As the light travels through space it becomes laterally coherent over a wider and wider region; that is, it will produce high-contrast Young fringes using a wider and wider separation of the double slits (Figure A.5.1).

If, however, the source slit is itself widened, the contrast of the Young fringes will fall because different points on the source now produce laterally displaced fringes. Because these source points are mutually noncoherent, the different fringe systems add in intensity, with a resulting blur (Figure A.5.2).

We *define* the state of partial coherence between the two Young slits

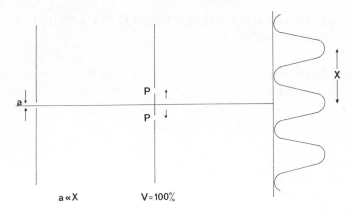

Figure A.5.1 A Young slit system with a small source slit giving sharp fringes. We define γ_{12} in terms of $V = [I_{max} - I_{min}]/[I_{max} + I_{min}]$.

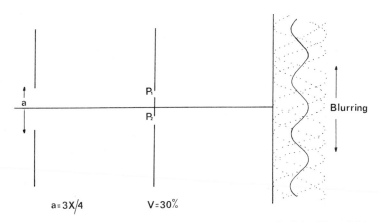

Figure A.5.2 A Young double slit system with a wider source slit giving blurred fringes of reduced contrast.

as the relative visibility of the fringe system. When this reaches zero, the Young slits are noncoherently illuminated. Van Cittert (1934) and Hopkins (1951) added a phase term to allow for lateral displacement of the fringes and to make the partial coherence coefficient complex. Today, the old term partial coherence has fallen into disuse and mutual coherence is preferred.

A.5.2.   RESPONSE OF A YOUNG SYSTEM TO A PERIODIC NONCOHERENT SOURCE

If instead of a single noncoherent slit, we use as a source an array of uniformly spaced noncoherent slits, the response of the Young system takes an interesting form. Should the source array subtend angles at the double slit with a basic repeat angular size that coincides with the angular size of the Young fringes, then a state of coincidence also occurs between the fringe systems produced by the individual slits in the composite noncoherent source. Although these fringe systems add in intensity, they nevertheless remain of high contrast because they are in register (Rogers 1963) (Figure A.5.3).

It will be seen, therefore, that a Young double slit can be used as a means of detecting a spatial frequency in a noncoherent source. The contrast of the fringes is proportional to the modulation depth of the particular spatial frequency, and their position to the phase.

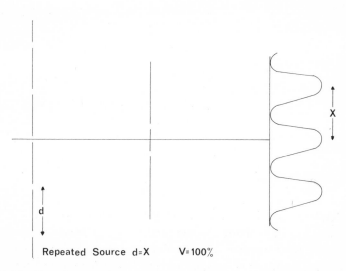

Repeated Source d=X   V=100%

Figure A.5.3 Noncoherent primary source now covered with multiple noncoherently related source slits with a regular spacing d = fringe width X. P_1 and P_2 are now coherently illuminated as visibility = 100%.

A.5.3. EVOLUTION OF THE SPATIAL FREQUENCY FILTER

A Young double slit system does not pass much light. It is a further modification of this idea that we may replace the Young double slit by a multiple slit system of uniform spacing. With the Young double slit the fringes are nonlocalized, but with the multiple Young slit they become localized. The plane of localization may be determined by geometrical optics, and the contrast of the fringes in this plane gives the modulation depth of the spatial frequency in the source. The lateral shift of fringes in this plane gives the phase of the input spatial frequency.

Having set up our geometrical model, all we have to do is to remove all reference to Youngs slits, interference, or monochromatic sources to get the spatial frequency filter of Figure 4.3.

This approach is of historical interest in that it is the way the author was led to set up his first spatial frequency filter.

A.5.4. IMAGING BY TESTING FOR PARTIAL COHERENCE

A Young double slit or a Young double pinhole system can be used to test a noncoherent source for the presence of a particular spatial frequency. If we use two pinholes of variable separation and variable

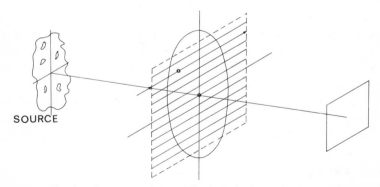

Figure A.5.4 The imaginary experiment. The lens is focused on an object, and an opaque plate carrying two pinholes is placed in front of it. This may or may not record Young interference fringes on the plate according to the degree of partial coherence at the pinholes. Repeat many thousands of times with pinholes in all possible pairs of positions to build up image. Alternatively, allow all pinholes to act simultaneously.

orientation to test spatial frequencies of all magnitudes and all orientations, we can put the information into a computer and calculate the object. Phase information is essential. We have, in effect, made a Fourier analysis of the source with the pinholes, and we use the computer to give us a Fourier synthesis. This is generally called the Zernike–Van Cittert theorem.

We could also use a sequential system of sampling pinholes in front of a lens (to correct the phases to a common zero) and build up an image by successive exposure to a plate (Figure A.5.4). More conveniently, we can use the lens to form an image by the simultaneous exposure of the plate to all bundles of rays entering its entrance pupil.

A.5.5.   THE ENTRANCE PUPIL FILTER

Suppose, for example, we wish to enhance a particular spatial frequency. Burch and Forno (1975) have used a camera in moire pattern work, in which they wished to form a good, high-contrast image of a rectangular net stuck on an engineering structure about to be deformed slightly. They, therefore, used a special entrance pupil stop consisting of two vertical slits and two horizontal slits whose spacing was "tuned" to the rectangular net they wished to image. This greatly increased the contrast of the image, and enabled good moire patterns to be obtained. The widths of the slits were such that one alone would pass the low spatial frequencies required to outline the object and locate the relatively broad moire fringes.

If the entrance pupil filter has more than two slits, the situation is more complex. In general, if there are N slits arbitrarily spaced they will pass selectively $\frac{1}{2}N(N-1)$ frequencies. It is, therefore, difficult to adjust the slit lengths to fit all the frequencies, but useful compromises can be effected. It is, for instance, possible to approximate to a Gaussian deblurring filter as shown in Chapter 10 (Rogers and Davies 1977).

REFERENCES

Burch, J. M. and C. Forno (1975). *Opt. Eng.* **14**, 178–185.
Hopkins, H. H. (1951). *Proc. Roy. Soc.* A **208**, 263.
Hopkins, H. H. (1953). *Proc. Roy. Soc.* A **217**, 408.

Mandel, L. and E. Wolf (1965). *Rev. Mod. Phys.* **37**, 231.

Rogers, G. L. (1963). *Proc. Phys. Soc. (GB)* **81**, 323–331.

Rogers, G. L. and J. C. Davies (1977). *Opt. Commun.* In press.

Van Cittert, P. (1934). *Physica* **1**, 201.

Van Cittert, P., (1939). *Physica* **6**, 1129.

Wolf, E. (1954). *Nuovo Cimento* **12**, 884.

Wolf, E., (1955). *Proc. Roy. Soc.* A **230**, 246.

Zernike, F., (1937a). *Zeits. Tech. Phys.* **18**, 568.

Zernike, F., (1937b). *Phys. Zeits.* **38**, 994.

Zernike, F., (1938). *Physics* **5**, 785–795.

Zernike, F., (1948). *Proc. Phys. Soc. (GB)* **61**, 158–164.

Author Index

Subject Index